How to Really Self-Publish Erotica

The Truth About Kinks, Covers, Advertising and More!

Dalia Daudelin

How to Really Self-Publish Erotica © 2013
by Dalia Daudelin

This edition of How to Really Self-Publish Erotica ©
2013 by Midnight Climax publishing

Cover photo © 2010 Photographer and Site.xxx
Interior layout and design by Nathan Holden

First Edition

ISBN-10 1492284092
ISBN-13 978-1492284093
Printed and distributed through CreateSpace, an
Amazon company

Midnight Climax

**If you enjoy this book, please rate and review it!
It influences what I will write next.**

Thank you for supporting indie erotica authors!

Visit Dalia Daudelin at DaliaDaudelin.com

Table of Contents

CHAPTER ONE
Introduction

Why You Should Write Erotica

The thing most people want in life is to make a lot of money for fairly little work. That's not exactly what this is, but it's damned close. If you want a reason to write erotica, there's none better.

After the success of *Fifty Shades of Gray*, the market exploded. A lot of people got very famous very quickly, and made a lot of money. Delilah Fawkes, for instance, was making six figures within a year. That was the gold rush, when people realized there was money to be made, 'gold in them hills' as it were. And flock to it they did.

The gold rush, I'm sorry to say, is over. You won't be getting rich. You'll probably be making less than full time at minimum wage, honestly, for a long time. Months. I wouldn't quit your job and buy your dream house until you know you can sustain it.

But honestly, that's good financial advice. I have had a few troubles in my career, which began in June 2012 (a little over a year ago as of the writing) and I made as much as 2,000 a month during that time, in spite of bad reviews and the fact that most of the information in this book wasn't handed to me. Of course, some was—I am not a pioneer. I walked a path that was fairly well-beaten, after the end of the gold rush. I had a wealth of information at my fingertips on the web, but at the same time so much information needed to come from practical experience and having done it ten, fifty, a hundred times.

If you've got a lucrative career, it might not seem like much. But frankly, I got out of high school with a 2.8 GPA, and no prospects for college. I worked for a year or two at a CVS, worked for three months at a Subway. In that time, I didn't make anywhere near what I have made in my time writing. And the job prospects just weren't coming either. I didn't have any friends in high places whispering in the right ears, I didn't know how to get people to just give me a chance, so it took me more than a year to get a job at all.
To me, after that, writing was a lifeline, and I appreciate it— even if I'm not going to be making $10,000 a month any time soon.

And what's more, the hours are short. Most writers, especially traditional writers, only write 2,000 words a day. Of course, working writers can turn the juice on and kick out 10,000 words a day or more. They CAN, but they rarely do so, because quite frankly it's very, very taxing. I'll get to that later, to a degree.
However, what that means on the other hand is that you have 3 or 4 hours of work a day, or less. That leaves quite a few

hours for going to the gym, spending time with the kids, browsing the web, catching up on your TV shows—you name it. Imagine if your commute time was zero, and you only worked a half-shift every single day. You can still take time off, of course.

Then of course you have the side benefits. You'll have experience writing. Everyone likes to say, 'I have an idea for a novel; maybe someday.' Frankly, they aren't going to write it. They don't know how to buckle down and get past the fact that their writing all seems to be coming out wrong. And when that happens, what are they going to do with their novel? Send it off to the Big Six and get turned down, or maybe offered a contract for half what it's worth? You will know how to get a story out there without any publisher taking a chunk of your money. You'll know how to push through the jittery starts and the bad days. And hell: maybe at the end of the day, when you're done with your erotica and you decide you've got an idea for a novel and you write it, maybe HarperCollins sends you an email telling you that they're real interested in the novel you published by yourself, would you like a deal to get it onto a shelf in Barnes and Noble. And along with that comes a nice fat check. Then you can say 'yes,' if you like. That's the dream, anyways.

What You Should Know (or, Why You Shouldn't Write Erotica)

The first thing that most people do when they start a new project is brag about it. For most people, that's just not going to happen for you. In fact, you'll probably spend a lot of your time avoiding talking in specifics about what you do.

The conversation seems to go like this:

Them: What do you do?
You: Oh, I'm a writer.
Them: That's cool! **What do you write about**?

That's when you suddenly realize that you write about the nastiest sex you can find, and there's no way in hell you want people you know reading it. Get your own preferred answer ready and get used to giving it. Mine is "it's nothing worth reading, but people pay for it, so it works."

Second, get used to the idea that you're never working hard enough. There's no real direct correlation between how much you write in a given day and how much money you make, but there IS a correlation between how many stories you have and your sales numbers. That means that in an ideal world, you'd be working 10 hours a day, writing 3000 words an hour or more. But you probably can't do that, nobody can.
Your limit isn't going to be the hours in the day any more, like it is in so many other jobs. It's going to primarily be your ability to focus on the task at hand. In an office job, there's a lot of making calls and talking to people, gathering information, etc. Once you get a knack for it, you can do it almost without thinking. Writers don't have any step on the line that isn't essentially thinking.
You have to constantly be thinking about your word choice. You have to constantly be deciding where you want your story to go if it's not outlined in advance. As much as everyone likes to talk a big game on outlines, when you're in the trenches things don't always go your way, so that'll be more

often than you like.

And what's more, what makes it ugly, is that when you're tired and you can't focus and you know in your head that your writing is suffering and you need to stop for the day—you'll have a little voice in your head (or a little external voice, sometimes!) pointing out that you're kicking off early. You could be working harder.

And then, at the end of the day, you're on the phone trying to explain to your sister in the least-specific words possible that you write nondescript fiction under a pen-name you don't care to mention, as if you're dealing drugs or something.

Lastly, be prepared for summer. In the publishing industry as a whole, including traditional big publishers like Random House as well as indie writers like myself and eventually you, regardless of genre, summer is a bad sales period. Your first summer, especially, is going to be demoralizing. The months I mentioned where I've made $2000? I made $1,000 last month. It's a damn lucky thing that I'm not reliant on publishing money to pay the rent at this point, I'll say that. But it's not just the incredible drops in money that you should expect. The thing that summer really does is demoralize you. You think, maybe it was a fluke, the readers don't like me anymore. A lot of writers quit because of bad sales, or panic. They need to be told: People don't buy books, or eBooks, in the summer. It's not you. It's the business.

But again—don't misunderstand me here. The money's fairly good, and the limits of your ability to be "on" and ready to work means you're probably going to be working less than 3 hours a day. All that comes at a cost, though, and I don't want to sound like it doesn't.

Principals in This Book

The first consideration, before you can discuss what to "do" is trying to figure out what your idea of success is, and trying to picture that in as specific a way as possible. The ultimate goal is to make enough money to keep your landlord happy, put food on the table, and have some left over at the end of the month to do something with. If you work hard, and you see sales, you'll see people who like the work you did.

So now we need to figure out how to get sales. "Isn't that what this book is about?" I hear you saying. It is, of course. But if I just claim something as true, you don't know how I figured it out, and you don't know how to figure it out for yourself if, for example, you think I'm wrong. Instead, I'm going to tell you where I get my ideas on the following subjects from:

Best sellers.

For the most part, I don't go looking for them, of course. I have been reading since I was in 3rd grade—I have a long history of seeing bestsellers on shelves, and for the most part I have to go looking for demonstrations of a point I know to be true from experience, rather than looking to figure out what my point *is*.

You're an independent publisher if you're selling eBooks through Amazon, through Kobo, and so on. You're not submitting to a publishing house, and that means you don't have all their experts. But we do know that they hire people and pay them to get results. In fact, their idea of results are the same results we want, namely sales.

When you see something that's consistent, a trend in publishing, you can assume it's probably not because the publisher really wants you (the reader) to benefit. It's because they want you to give them your money, and it is in their best interest to do whatever it takes to win you over. Even if, as it happens, the way to win you over is by helping you. Or hurting you.

So, where possible, I'll try to back up my discussion points with examples from multi-time bestselling authors' printed work. Because that's where publishers are spending their money.

This Book Is Wrong

Of course, I could be wrong. There are a lot of things I can easily see, off the top of my head, that are obviously flawed (or potentially flawed) about my premise here.

First, I'm fairly negative about the idea that writers are first-and-foremost "artists" with "artistic vision." Are writers artists? Oh, certainly. But they do it with a specific monetary impetus. At least in my case, I don't feel that it empowers me to make decisions that I like, but are objectively bad. At least, not when there's money at stake.

But you know what? That's just me. If you think it's not about the money or, even better, you think that an artistic perspective will bring you more money? I absolutely encourage you to tell me I'm wrong about my motivation. Please, do read the rest of the book, you might learn a few things even though you disagree with my motives, but you don't have to think I'm right about everything.

You might think that being emotionally distanced from my work hurts my ability to tell a compelling story. I'd certainly agree there are cases where I think that's happened. But let me discuss for a moment my fiancé.

He's a reader. Takes the bus to class, and reads on the bus. Last semester, he started reading this novel, *Under the Eagle* by Simon Scarrow. I've read the reviews, and it's frankly very clear that Mr. Scarrow is "doing it for the money." The beau knows this; when I mentioned it, he said something along the lines of 'yeah, of course he's only doing it for the money.' Does that mean that when he finished *Under the Eagle,* he didn't pick up *The Eagle's Conquest*? That is not what it meant.

I don't think that the fact that there's a clear motive beyond artistic merit hurts a story's ability to be strong. In fact, it's absolutely imperative for profit to occur, that you convince a sufficiently large group of people that your story is worth paying for, and you convince them on the back of strong artistic work.

How to Be Right

There are a number of people who don't follow the crowd and are successful. And, for that matter, there are a number of people who make good decisions and aren't as successful as they would like. There's a good deal of luck involved, but nobody is successful as a result of their bad decisions (though some are a success because of good decisions, in spite of other blatant bad decisions).

I've tried to use examples that are not only successful, but representative of very standard middle-of-the-road success. People who made solid decisions that I would recommend anyone make. On the other hand, there are a lot of people who are successful and made different decisions.

I'd encourage anyone who disagrees, to try to do whatever they think is right. Use examples you think are better examples as a source of inspiration and guidance. But first and foremost, make sure you're looking at someone who was actually successful, who had results you want to have. If they can do it, you can do it. But if they couldn't do it, then it may not be a matter of effort or talent. It may be that they made bad decisions that hurt their career and will hurt your career if you let them.

So if and when you decide you want to get your own selection of exemplary work, look at whatever you think is best, but at the same time, make sure you look at people who went where you want to go.

CHAPTER TWO
The Process of Writing

Word Processing Programs

There are three classes of word processors that I see commonly being used by authors with whom I've had conversations about that sort of thing.

The most common by far are people who use "WYSIWYG" word processors, almost always as part of a suite of programs. In this market there are a few major competitors, although almost all of them are widely comparable.

Microsoft Word, part of their *Office* suite of programs, this is the best-known Word Processor that you have to pay for. The price can lead to a bit of sticker shock, though; Office is now only available as a periodical service for $10 a month or $100 a year. This is perhaps the most useful of the programs, though, because their native format is .doc (.docx now, but with legacy support for .doc) which is the only format accepted at all major eBook retailers.

More accessible are free suites, OpenOffice.Org being the

best-known of them. It's developed and maintained by Sun Microsystems, the same guys who developed Java.

After a disagreement about software copyright, some of the developers left and created LibreOffice, using some code from OpenOffice. There's a lot of similarity, and the primary distinction is in the politics of the situation. If you don't care about that, OpenOffice is more popular.

There are many people who choose to use "distraction-free" processors, which are designed to allow the user to work in an environment devoid of colorful icons, and often are used in full-screen to remove the temptation of Twitter or Facebook, which are the bane of so many writers.

There are literally dozens of examples of this type of software, and none of them are objectively better or worse than others.

The most popular and, according to many, the best is WriteRoom. In general, WriteRoom is the first 'distraction-free' editor most people learn about, though it is only available for Macintosh computers.

The relative simplicity of the software, though, has led to many different developers making comparable software.

I have personally used Write or Die Desktop Edition, FocusWriter, Q10, ZenEdit, ZenWriter, and DarkRoom in no particular order. My personal preference is for Write or Die, though my fiancé enjoyed ZenWriter during his time with it last semester. The differences are few, and the ones that can't be adjusted to meet a preference are fewer. The choice for Windows users generally comes down purely to preference.

Thirdly are, what I would call, "organizers." The most popular and the best is Scrivener. In fact, I am currently writing this in Scrivener. I try to be fairly stingy when so many wonderful free options exist, but Scrivener and Write or Die are two pieces of software I find that I cannot do without. Scrivener is an indispensable tool for larger projects, including research papers and longer works.

For shorter works, less than 10,000 words, I often find that there aren't enough ideas at work in the story to require external structure.

There are, of course, alternatives. There's Liquid Story Binder, which I absolutely cannot recommend: it's very unattractive for modern software, and doesn't work as intuitively as Scrivener.

There's also the software by the creator of the Snowflake method, Snowflake Pro, which I have not used. The method is effective, but the software may or may not be; I have no way of knowing.

While other opinions are available, I prefer to write in Write or Die, since the time limit function (one of the few things that differentiates it from the others—I almost didn't mention it in that list) works so effectively to focus my thoughts. For longer works I will often work in Scrivener, even though it lacks that functionality, because the organizational tools are too for me to pass up.

Issues of Style

There are things that are important to consider outside of the fetishistic content in your story. However, many of them are simply guidelines, and no reference is needed in the long run. So while there will almost certainly be more diversity here, it's likely to be a relatively short section.

First, on length. Longer stories tend to sell better for the same price. Of course, on the other hand, you take longer to recoup the invested time that you have spent, and considering that you have to spend real dollars on stock and possibly advertising, there are possible risks to that approach (which is why you don't see people releasing full-length novels in the area of 50,000 words for $2.99).

With that in mind, the bare minimum in this market is 3,000 words. Many authors I know strive to write around 15,000. I tend to write between 3 and 5,000. I don't know that it hurts my sales, per se. My single longer story is not a better seller than my short stories.

Sex scene length is important. There is, in theory, such a thing as a sex scene that's too long: Like video pornography, it's defined by the point when people pack up and go home because they're finished. I have only read one story where the scene was so long that I was actually annoyed by it, and it went on for almost 10,000 words. I am not exaggerating: From the time the girls walked into the room and started taking their clothes off in the same paragraph, until they were falling asleep and talking about how good it was, TEN THOUSAND words. Every time I thought the sex was over, it moved on to another phase. Lesbians, what can I say?

That said, you're not likely to write a ten thousand word block of pure lesbian sex. And I read it all. I was finished halfway through. I read it because it was in the middle of a 21,000 word pseudo-romance, which ended with TWO EPILOGUES (another 1200 and 1500 words, respectively) that tied it up into a legitimate romance with a nice happy ending. It was a good story, sits at the top of Literotica's Lesbian-category Hall of Fame as of this writing, and it was much too long for my liking when I was trying to get off but I really appreciated it afterward.

Until you can write 10,000 words of sex scene, assume that longer is always going to be better. Then write it long because balancing that behemoth scene out with story is going to put you in the 20,000 word range and you're going to see absurdly good sales from a long story like that (which you should price according to the amount of work you put in—I'd recommend $4.99 or more).

Tone is a tricky subject, because a lot of it is tied up in the voice of the narrator. With that said, there are a lot of things that are going to distance the reader from the story, going to essentially hurt the mood you're trying to create.

First, I mentioned it in the section on BDSM, but don't portray sadists. Even if you understood sadism, and you could portray it, the entire thing is a losing battle, since it's so cerebral. There's nothing sexual to an outsider about sadism— it's not sweet or romantic. It's distant and controlled and people can't *really* get off on that.

On the other end of the spectrum, there is a range where tone is too relaxed and too playful. I've seen many stories by people who were not professional writers, where they say things like "I was harder than Chinese algebra" and it's a cute, if overused, metaphor... but it's a joke.

Erotica, like sex, is all about tension, sexual tension, that builds until the sex scene; then the character's desire to orgasm provides the tension, and gives the reader something to substitute their own desires in for. Making jokes is a way

to release tension, and that's not something you want to
be doing, certainly not lightly. Try to maintain a relatively
professional, level-headed tone. Obviously this isn't a medical
description of sexuality (unless it is) but you don't want
someone wisecracking all over your story—use discretion.
At the same time, especially in the modern audience, the old
flowery language is frowned on. One film, making a joke
at the expense erotica writers, used the phrase 'Undulating
with desire, Adrian removes her crimson cape, at the site of
Reginald's stiff and tumescent…' The script leaves it hanging
at that point, but it's clear what is to come. There is certainly,
even today, a certain stigma attached to the genre because of
the purple prose of days past.

Now you can afford to use words like 'hard cock' fairly
easily, and if you're saying *penis* so often that you run out
of relatively standard terms and descriptions, you may be
overdoing it. Remember that as in all writing, it's always
smarter to describe in fewer words if it gets the same meaning
across—instead of an intellectual understanding of what you
mean they tend to get more of a general idea, which tends to
be easier to internalize, and therefor, to feel in their gendered
bits.

As a final note, it's a bit of a tricky subject, but a trap many
beginning writers fall into is that of trying to control what the
reader sees in their head too much.

You are not a continuity manager on a film set, trying to
make sure every detail is correct. You don't need to explain
how actions are performed in explicit detail. He can 'take her
breast in his hand' without having to 'take her left breast in
his right hand.' It may seem silly to some, but this is a much
more common problem than it should be. It very quickly takes

a genre that's easy to slip into the rut of inserting tab A into slot B, and drives it to the mechanical description as if that was the main selling point.

Titling

There's a certain art to titling stories, and there is no level where there's sufficient talent. I try to encourage a level of working proficiency, where you are trying to make money even though you will probably know full well that you're not giving a product that is ideal. The work will make you better over time; there's no reason to waste time on "practice" unless you're doing it for your own enjoyment.

Titling is where the rubber meets the road on this. In writing, often I go without heavy editing (it's led to problems in the past, actually) but in titling the first idea I have is almost never very good. This is one of the few places where my fiancé and I tend to collaborate because titling is not easy.

You want to capture the tone of the story first and foremost. But you also want to make it very clear from the title that this is erotic fiction. There are some times when this is less true, especially when blurring the lines between genres, but for the most part your early work should be porn in the truest sense, and your titles should reflect that.

"Lesbian Psycho Dramas 3" is probably a bit too direct, but at the same time "the Land of the Free" might be a bit too indirect. Words like 'Pleasure' and 'Love' are easy targets that don't go too far, and then for more specific situations it can also become clearer. For example, my story "Bratty Babysitters get Spankings." It's very clear what's happening, without being excessively vulgar. That balance is important to maintain even when it seems like it's a little silly.

One major exception, listed above, is in cases where the focus isn't on the erotica. In these places, you can afford a more abstract title, like my title "Monarch Mind," where the focus is on MK-ULTRA brainwashing rather than penises. The other is where there is no focus on any sort of story at all, and it's all pornographic. For example, my story "Kinky Public Gang Bang." There's a story, and I could tell it to you, but it'd be short without the sex. It essentially boils down to this: Instead of "I met a guy once, and we had sex," the story was "I'm going to tell you about sex I had once."
Once again, the title directly reflected the experience that the reader should have expected. That's why I was fairly explicit: the story was equally vulgar.

Bundles

Of special note are bundles. Bundles are absolutely, one-hundred percent, where your money is made. There may be other stories that have better sales numbers, but bundles sell on much higher margin, and have nearly infinitely less work involved.

Realistically, your time is not free. You can pretend it is, and many authors and self-employed people do, but it's unfair to you and it's unfair to your customers. If you price at a fairly reasonable 10 cents a word, then your writing, for a three-thousand word piece, is worth $30.
Add minimum wage for the hour you'll spend on designing a cover, formatting the story, and uploading to all your storefronts, and you're talking about $38 for a story. Now add $2 for cover stock, and we round off to an easy $40 that you spent on producing one short story, which can be done in a

day or two.

The market price for such a story is $2.99. This is the minimum price to get the seventy percent royalty, and the standard for erotic short fiction. I did not choose this price; you did not choose this price. This is the most we can afford to charge, and this is a luxury market, so lower prices don't mean better sales; they often mean a customer will think the goods are inferior.

At seventy percent royalty, on every single sale you make $2.10. To make up the cost of writing, producing, and publishing your story, you need to sell 19 units to make back the money you've already "spent."

There is, however, a bigger cost of writing, which should be paid careful attention when you're still in the early stages. You need to consider your library and what is selling well, because every time you write any story, that can be your best-seller if you target it right.

Most of the time it won't be, of course. But your time isn't just being spent in terms of writing, it's also being spent in terms of not-writing. Don't think that you can't work on personal projects, but don't do something half-assed when the money's what you really want.

You could have spent another twenty minutes on conceptualizing and made more money over the next six months. Decide if you've spent enough time considering if the sales will be strong with your current idea before you go off and running with it.

However, bundles are work that has already been done. There is no opportunity cost associated with the content of a bundle, like there is with individual short stories. Your choice was only to bundle or not, rather than to write a different bundle that might sell better. Therefore, what you have is only that $8 from the hour of designing a cover, producing a book, and publishing it, and the $2 of stock—if you don't know what I mean, I promise we will get to it. In short, I'm referring to images to use on your cover.

In addition, because there is realistically more content in a bundle, it's priced accordingly. The standard price price is $7 for a bundle of three or four stories; therefor at seventy percent the royalty is $4.90. With the sale of only two bundles, you've already made up the cost of production, less twenty cents.

There is absolutely no reason not to bundle. The only question is: "how should bundles be made in order to sell the best they can?"

The first option you have is to write a series. Three serial short stories are ideal for bundling, and encourage readers to buy on the basis that they'll get a complete story, plenty of sexual enjoyment out of your bundle. Over time, even if the story may be lacking, readers might be able to develop interest in these characters.

When a series is not ideal, or when you've got a story that's self-contained, then the next best thing to a series is a bundle built around a single subject that ties stories together. Kinks are perhaps the best way to tie a set of stories together, though certain elements of milieu (historical, especially) can be used to create a tie between all the stories.

However, once you've got all your series stories bundled, and you've got all of your related materials bundled into groups of three, there's still a very real likelihood that there will be multiple stories left over.

For these, I like to recommend the "grab bag" bundle, which promises a sample of different stories. Readers can buy it and instead of getting a concentrated shot of three incest stories, they get a taste test of incest, DubCon, and billionaires to see what ultimately tickles their fancy.

Ultimately, the general idea is to keep in mind that you need to sell these stories to a consumer, so when you have any bundle you want to understand the idea that you're going to sell to the customer.

The Editing Process

There's a thousand quotes out there about editing. A lot of them are really neat little things. Let me boil them all down, and take the fun out of them for you:

Mostly, delete words.

There are a few very specific examples where you're going to be adding words to a 2nd draft, but not most of them. Most of the time, you're wasting your words and if you had an editor he'd be removing words, sentences, paragraphs that add nothing to your story.

My process is fairly simple, and I think most people could adopt it. It's not the only one out there, but it's one of the least complicated. A day or two after you finish your draft, sit down with it. Every time you have a thought other than 'this is good,' it needs to be deleted or changed. If the entire paragraph structure falls apart without that sentence or phrase, change it to make more sense. If removing it changes little or nothing, then remove it.

Often when I finish a first draft and print it out for editing, there is not a single paragraph that doesn't have major revisions.

The importance of an edit and a 2nd draft cannot be overstated, though for many of my titles I find that my priorities don't necessitate an edit. The importance of a 3rd draft is debatable, and an author whose money is made in bulk may want to skip it. After all, editing is something that can be done essentially forever; nothing is perfect, and you'll always find changes you want to make, so editing can be very time consuming, and this becomes more true the longer the work. A 4th draft should only be necessary if there were major structural changes in the 2nd or 3rd drafts.

CHAPTER THREE
The Process of Selling

Blurb

As a reader, there are only five things you know about a story
when you see it on Amazon: The title, the author's name, the
description, the cover, and *maybe* you have heard someone
else discuss it, so you would have their opinion. The saying
goes "don't judge a book by its cover," but in all fairness there
is precious little else that a person can judge by.

Without knowing anything in advance about the author, and
without knowing anything in advance about the book, the
reader has to figure out from the copy, the title, and the cover
whether or not this book is going to interest them, and how
it compares to other books that compete not only for their
dollars but for their limited time. Right now, there are 97,000
erotic books and stories on the Kindle store. If you read 5 of
them a day you would still take more than 50 years to read
them all, and in that time their number would have more than
doubled. Your titling ability and your cover design are going
to open the door, but your blurbs are going to have to seal the
deal.

As an author just starting out, you cannot rely on a reputation, you cannot rely on reviews, you cannot rely on recommendations and endorsements. All of those things are very important, and in time you will develop them. However, with all of the endorsements in the world, people will not buy a title that doesn't have anything going for it.

Titling and covers will be discussed elsewhere. The blurb, however, is one of the things that I routinely see done improperly, and one of the easiest places to improve for almost any writer. It's an important tool that the publishing industry has proliferated to do exactly what you want it to do: Tell the reader why they want to read your story.

There's a lot of space in stories of all genres that is used on important, but non-essential material. Certainly, Jon Snow's strained relationship with Catelyn Stark is important to his character, it informs his entire worldview. But if we were to tell the story of Jon Snow so that it was as short as possible but complete, we wouldn't even mention his step-mother. The blurb is a way to get to the essential core of what your story is about, and tell your readers what that is.

Most erotica writers have a blurb in two parts: The copy, and then the advertisement.

Take this sample from my book, *A Rape Fantasy*:

A crash defiles a silent night. A man defiles a beautiful wife.

A serene night turns into a series of terrible events when

an intruder breaks into a married woman's home. With her husband away, she's left alone and unprotected, vulnerable to the man's strength and violent lust. When she comes face to face with one of her deepest, darkest fantasies, she has no choice but to give in.

Will her body betray her? Will she come to enjoy this kinky fantasy she's kept to herself all these years?

This 3000 word erotic short includes graphic scenes of forced sex and light BDSM.

The first 3 sections—I hesitate to call them paragraphs—are all setting the stage for the story. That's what the advertising industry calls 'copy writing.'
On the other hand, the last section-paragraph is an element that is somewhat unique to eBook pornography: We're just telling the reader what they're getting, without any story-based pitch at all. Between the two, we're assuming that people want to read something arousing to them, and therefore they want to know what sort of sex will be occurring, but that it's subject to the story.

There's a very fine balance to maintain when writing your description. There are different levels of description required by different retailers: Smashwords requires less than 400 characters for their "short" description, which is the primary one shown to your readers. That means that you need to get your description very short: after you include your tagging at the end, you will only have one or two sentences to describe your story. It's not quite a tweet, but it's close.

However, frankly, the majority of your money will not be coming from Smashwords. I make, consistently, over $1000 a month in the slowest months. A year ago at this time I was making $200 a month. Yet, from Smashwords I make barely $500 per quarter. Realize of course that I receive royalty checks from multiple sources, and even my biggest distributors really don't account for all of my monthly income.

So for the most part, I prefer to try to keep in mind that most of my money's not made on my 400 character short description, it's made from my Amazon descriptions or my Barnes and Noble descriptions.

If you go into a store and pick up a fat hardcover, you might find something like the dust jacket description of Twilight, which clocks in at 170 words. It's not the longest blurb I've read, not even the longest for a best-seller.

Pay special attention here to three things: Introduction to the heroine, setting the mood, and setting the scene for the story.

I'd never given much thought to how I would die -- though I'd had reason enough in the last few months -- but even if I had I would not have imagined it like this ... surely it was a good way to die, in the place of someone else, someone I loved. Noble, even. That ought to count for something.

When Isabella Swan moves to the gloomy town of Forks, and meets mysterious, alluring Edward Cullen, her life takes a thrilling and terrifying turn. With his porcelain skin, golden eyes, mesmerizing voice, and supernatural gifts, Edward is both irresistible and impenetrable. Up

until now, he's managed to keep his true identity hidden, but Bella is determined to uncover his dark secret.

What Bella doesn't realize is the closer she gets to him, the more she is putting herself and those around her at risk. And, it might be too late to turn back ...

Deeply seductive and extraordinarily suspenseful, Twilight will have readers riveted right until the very last page is turned.

There's a lot of stuff here. It can be fairly split after the first paragraph—in fact, there is a divider on the jacket. Then the last paragraph is just trying to sell the thing without adding almost anything. This is essentially the same thing that you're going to be doing with your tagging sentence(s).

Compare that blurb, now, to something much terser from the back of a paperback copy of Louis L'Amour's *Heller With A Gun*. The Western genre is a niche market, so it's not a best-seller, but on the other hand it's a consistent market, perhaps even more so than Fantasy/Sci-Fi. It's actually a very good analogue for erotica, outside of outliers like *Fifty Shades*. That blurb is only 83 words, but even still manages to evoke an understanding in the reader of what they're going to receive in their story.

It was a hard land that bred hard men to hard ways. King Mabry survived by his guns. He wasn't proud of his deadly skill, nor was he ashamed. He just lived with it every hard day on the frontier. When a traveling theatrical

troupe hired a ruthless killer to guide them through the Wyoming wilderness, King Mabry -- his guns at the ready -- set out to follow their trail, and not blizzards, not Indians, nor the wily guide would stop them.

Now look there, and we again have an early tone establisher. The entire thing drips pulpy Western. We meet the hero, we find out what his goals are. I think, personally, that the blurb here reflects somewhat the fact that it's a better-conceived story than Twilight. I'm not the first to point out: it's essentially a story about a girl who has no real direction or goals in her life.
This is a story about a man whose goals are self-determined. Even though in the same way it seems to imply a (probably romantic) response to meeting someone new, it suggests agency where Twilight's blurb implies that Bella is basically driftwood on the torrential river of Edward.

Now compare those two, written by professional copy editors, to a Western description—to keep things comparable—from FictionPress, where the descriptions are limited to 384 characters. Mind that this is the most favored story in the category, *Untamable* by R.M. Whitaker:

Both fear and curiosity fill Mercedes McBride when her father requests that she return to live with him in Texas at the end of the Civil War. What she never dreamed was that she might find love on the wildest adventure of her entire life in the old West..

We've got a lot less room, and this is not professional copy.

It's much shorter than either, thanks to the limitations of FictionPress, only 50 words (though they have 134 spare characters). There's not much impression of tone here, so that's a strike against it. However, we've met the heroine, we know her situation, and we know something about the story. There's room for improvement, certainly. There's no clue what sort of adventure is occurring—is this *Once Upon a Time in the West* adventure, or *Two Mules for Sister Sara* adventure? Is she going to be an action-girl? We don't know. We could be told, but there's also a strong implication that the entire adventure is a surprise, so it would make some sense to be as much a surprise to the reader as to the heroine.

Now to finish up, let's look at page 11 on the "most favorited" list, for *Origins* by Drucilla:

The origins of the horrors in the desert

What? There's nothing here at all. We are told in 8 words only the most limited possible information about the story. Based on this information we know: There is a horror in the desert. We are going to be told its origins. What is a "horror?" Perhaps they mean a Lovecraftian horror. So is this a crossover, or should I expect something more akin to *The Colour Out Of Space*? Is it more *Deadlands* or *Cowboys vs Aliens*? It's unknown, and unknowable.

Uploading

AMAZON

Amazon (https://kdp.amazon.com) is the biggest storefront for digital books in most English-speaking countries. If you have to skip a website when you're uploading your stories, make sure it's not Amazon. You will probably get most of your money every month from Amazon.

However, Amazon is perhaps the most finicky of the websites, so there's a few things to keep in mind. At the top of the uploading page, there's an option to enroll your title in KDP Select. There are a few considerations here, and we'll get into those later: they're fairly complex, and right now we're just dealing with the basics. If you're not sure you know what you're doing, err on the side of caution and don't enroll your book in Select.

Secondly, there's a box there for "Search keywords." These are **very** important. These 7 keywords are how your book will be found through outside search engines like Google or Bing. You want to make sure you choose keywords that will maximize your sales. A helpful tool to get you on the right track is the Google Keyword Tool (http://www.googlekeywordtool.com/).

Additionally, these keywords are used to get into certain categories. For example, there is a category, Romance > Lesbian Romance (that is to say, 'Lesbian Romance' in 'Romance') that you cannot select on your own. Instead, you can add "Lesbian" as a keyword, and then choose any other Romance sub-category, and your work will automatically show up in Lesbian Romance as well.

A word of caution about categories; if you choose the Erotica category, then any other category you choose will be ignored. So there is an advantage in not putting your story in the Erotica category.

Amazon pays monthly, 60 days after the end of the month. So, what you make in June will usually be paid by the end of September, but possibly as late as the beginning of October. Keep in mind that you have to make $10, £10, and €10 minimum. If you don't meet the minimum for a given currency, it won't pay out until the month when you do. So, if you make $9 in June, and $2 in July, you'd have $11 paid out at the end of October.

BARNES AND NOBLE
Barnes and Noble (https://www.nookpress.com) is the other big name in self-publishing. I make almost as much here as I do on Amazon, but it took me longer to start making good money here at all. Sales are a bit less consistent, but you have a lot more room to write more taboo content, which generally will produce more sales if you're willing to not distribute to Amazon or elsewhere. They accept literal incest, instead of pseudo-incest, as well as bestiality.
On this website, you get 5 categories to put your book in. Use them all! Be aware, however, that they do require a smaller image than Amazon; I recommend 1300x1900. Just resize the larger cover image you would upload to any other distributor and you should be fine.
Barnes and Noble pays monthly, 60 days after each month, similar to Amazon. However, unlike Amazon, they don't have a minimum payment amount.

KOBO
Kobo (https://writinglife.kobobooks.com) is a smaller website, but they're growing fast. I make probably a third of what I make on Amazon through Kobo sales, so don't rely on them for your bread and butter, but they absolutely do bring in money. Kobo is popular outside the US, so expect most of your sales

to be from Canada, the UK, and Australia. If you're uploading a book for $2.99—which I absolutely recommend you do— then be sure to manually set the British Pound price to £1.99, or else you won't be making your full 70% commission.

Keep in mind, however, Kobo requires a smaller cover image like Barnes and Noble, rather than the larger Amazon cover. Kobo pays 45 days following the month where you earn $100. If you make $150 in January, then you're going to be paid $150 on March 15. However, if in February you only make $60, and then in March you only make $60 again, then you won't be receiving a check in April, but in May you'll receive a check for $120.

SMASHWORDS

Smashwords (https://www.smashwords.com) is, first and foremost, the gateway to the iTunes store. They upload to a number of other web sites, including Barnes and Noble and Kobo, as well as other sites, but the iTunes store is a closed door to anyone who's not working on a Mac.

Publishing through Smashwords is fairly easy, but afterward there are a few important steps to take. From the Dashboard, choose ISBN manager from the left-side bar. This is where you'll get a free ISBN from Smashwords, which is an absolute necessity for certain vendors to be willing to distribute your work.

After that, you want to open the Channel Manager, which is also on the left-side bar. This is where you'll be able to choose which storefronts you want your story to be available through. Opt-out of Amazon, since they won't be uploading to Amazon in spite of the option being there. Also opt-out of any store that you'd rather upload to yourself.

Remember, Smashwords pays quarterly rather than monthly. If you'd rather get paid more often from any place that you can upload to manually or have Smashwords do it for you, then opt-out and upload the story manually.

OTHER

Of course, those aren't your only options. Those are the four ways I choose to release my stories, but that's a personal choice that I've made.

All Romance eBooks (http://www.allromanceebooks.com/) is only interested in romance, though you can certainly turn up the steaminess there! Another good option is Rainbow eBooks (http://www.rainbowebooks.com/) if you want to be sure to get your books to as many distributors as possible—note that they only deal with LGBT fiction.

Draft2Digital (https://www.draft2digital.com) is another website that can be very useful as a possible alternative to Smashwords; D2D will upload your books to Amazon, Barnes and Noble, Kobo, and the iTunes store, but they don't have their own storefront like Smashwords does, and not quite as wide a variety of distributors.

Keep in mind, this list can't ever be truly complete, because new distributors are going to come and go over the years, and some of them might be very good but we can't predict what hasn't happened yet. Even if it's not on this list, it might be good.

As a last thought, make sure that you're not uploading your copyrighted works and giving your bank account information to a scam website trying to trick unsuspecting authors out of their money. Check with other authors: if nobody else has used it, it's probably not safe. You should avoid taking that kind of risk. Only trust websites that you can verify are legitimate.

Advertising

Advertising is the number one thing self publishers are interested in. This is partially because traditional publishers focus heavily on advertising for their blockbuster books, and partly because we're told again and again that advertising is the most important step of publishing.

You're not a traditional publisher, though, and it's time to stop thinking that you are. You don't have a million dollars to spend on tours and paid reviewers. Traditional publishers are also known for buying their way onto bestseller lists, as detailed on Forbes (http://www.forbes.com/sites/jeffbercovici/2013/02/22/heres-how-you-buy-your-way-onto-the-new-york-times-bestsellers-list/). If you don't have the money to buy thousands of copies of your book, or to buy a spot on a TV show, you can't think like a traditional publisher.

Furthermore, there is something more important than advertising: writing your next book. Your next book will point more people to your work than any tweet on Twitter or post on FaceBook ever will. Social media is a great way to keep fans engaged, but it's not ideal for making new ones.

If you're ever asking yourself if you should devote more time to writing or to social media, choose to devote more time to writing. The more books you have in your catalog, the higher your odds of being discovered by a reader. Erotica readers are voracious, and they are actively searching for books like yours to read.

With that being said, there **are** a few effective ways to get new readers as well as maintain fans for an ever-growing fan base that will buy most of your books.

Mailing Lists

With my first pen name, I never had a mailing list. In fact, I didn't pick one up until I was on my tenth book on my fourth pen name! I'll put it mildly: waiting was a mistake. Do yourself a favor. If you're serious about writing erotica, go out right now and get a PO box so you can set up a mailing list before you publish your first book.

People sign onto your mailing lists if they like your work and want to read more of it. Utilize that! I've seen authors recommend that you give free copies of every one of your books to mailing list subscribers. I don't do that, but at sign up they do get a free copy of a book and I might occasionally send out my newest one to readers.

I send out an email to my list about once a week, depending on what I release that week. I tell them what new stories I have up, asking them for honest reviews and maybe a push on What To Read After Fifty Shades of Grey (discussed later). To do this, I use mailchimp.com, one of the easiest ways to manage a mailing list.

I told you to get a PO box because by law you have to include an address in the footer of your emails. If you don't mind using your real address, then that's fine too, but for added privacy do use a PO box. They're cheap and might come in handy if you ever have fans who want to send you something. On my mailing list I regularly have 80% of my readers who click through to my links. Many of them go on to buy the books I'm advertising. I imagine you can see how valuable a resource that could be if you use it correctly.

Social Media

If you enjoy using Twitter, Facebook, or Tumblr, then by all means use them. I'm obsessed with my personal Tumblr, in fact! But these accounts are not likely to bring you a new fan or convince someone to buy your books. To get fans interested in following you, too, you must be original. You can't only post links to your work, you must talk to others, be witty, offer something valuable to them.

Any time readers are asked how they find books, word of mouth is number one. You never see Twitter or Facebook mentioned at all, or within the top 10 ways readers find books. Social media just isn't a reliable way to get new eyes on your work.

There are some services selling advertising on these sites. Don't waste your money. These might be helpful for some other genres, but they're not useful for erotica authors.

Blogs

I run a blog. I don't post much on it right now, though I did have plans that I just never followed through on. But if you're running a blog and all you post is links to your books, no one's going to want to read it. People don't subscribe to blogs because they really love advertisements, they subscribe to blogs because they offer something the person wants to read. Maybe you could blog about politics, or the self publishing world, or something other than just HEY READ MY BOOKS!

Even just blogging about your life is better than just blogging about your books. You could post photos of your animals, photos from vacations, talk about your thoughts and feelings. These are the kinds of things that make for successful blogs. If you're a mom, you could be a self publishing mommy blogger.

Or you could write about the process of writing, or post whatever research you do for your stories to your blog. There's plenty you can do with such an open platform, so be creative with it.

Reviews

In 2012, reviews got a lot of bad press. It suddenly came out that some of the biggest author names had been paying for reviews, and that this practice was surprisingly common. Suddenly the business of reviewing crashed, big names had to issue formal apologies, thousands of reviews were deleted from Amazon, and the terms of service on Amazon changed. Now if you are an author it's hard to have your reviews go live, because they will be under much more scrutiny. Even if a review is legitimate, they might be deleted by a paranoid Amazon admin.

However, what we did learn is that, for the small fries at least, reviews don't really change sales much. Sure, you're probably more likely to make a sale with 5 stars than a 1 star, but if the reviews are fake readers are going to know it.

There are still some people out there selling reviews. Do yourself a favor, save yourself the money and the headache, and don't buy them. You can get reviews legitimately by starting a mailing list and sending free copies of your books to those who subscribe. If you ask these fans for reviews, they're much more likely to give them than a random customer would.

Paid Advertising

I've used paid advertisements in the past, and I can't recommend them. Not until you have 30 or more books. It might work, it might not, but it's really not worth it either way when there are so many other options that are free. In my experiments with paid advertising, I've tried using Google ads, Facebook ads, and ads on Reddit. None of these have made me any sales at all, even with my large catalog. Stick to the mailing list and the advertising that I'll detail in the next chapters.

Facebook

There are two free Facebook pages that allow erotica authors to advertise their work. There are more, but What To Read After Fifty Shades of Grey (WTRAFSOG) (https://www.facebook.com/WhatToReadAfter50ShadesOfGrey) and Korner Kafe Exposed (http://www.facebook.com/KornerKafeX) are two of the most popular. Unlike paid advertisements, I find that there's little risk in submitting your work to either of these sources, and I've had pretty good success getting sales as a result of being posted there. They each have their own forms to submit to have the stories featured.

The form to submit to WTRAFSOG is here at **http://tinyurl.com/lq84wol**.

The form to submit to Korner Kafe Exposed is at **http://tinyurl.com/k29c6g7**.

For the synopsis, you would put in the story's blurb.

Then it asks for the 10 digit ASIN for Amazon.com. This is probably the trickiest part of the whole deal; if you scroll down on the Amazon page for the eBook, you'll find the Product Details section which will look like this:

Product Details

File Size: 156 KB

Print Length: 19 pages

Simultaneous Device Usage: Unlimited

Publisher: Midnight Climax (July 12, 2013)

Sold by: Amazon Digital Services, Inc.

Language: English

ASIN: B00DX0KZOK

Text-to-Speech: Enabled ⌄

X-Ray: Not Enabled ⌄

Lending: Enabled

In the example image I've given here, for my book *Take Me*, the number we're looking for is B00DX0KZOK. Note here that there are both zeroes and letter 'O's. The O is more round, but you can also just copy-and-paste.

The WTRAFSOG form then asks for the print copy's ISBN. If it has a print copy available, go ahead and add that. If not, feel free to leave that section blank.

If your story is going to be free for a period, you can add the dates it will be free in the next section.

On the WTRAFSOG form, it then asks for reader comments. This is where you can put comments on the book or any other info you think readers should have. Since the Korner Kafe

Exposed form doesn't have that section, you can add those comments to the beginning of the synopsis.

Give it a few days and hopefully your book will be posted to those Facebook pages, and with a little luck, you'll see a huge spike in sales. Once when I used WTRAFSOG, I had 80 sales for a brand new book overnight. That's the kind of effect that a successful advertisement can have, and that's the kind of result we're looking for.

Free

Giving away books for free has been a popular form of advertising for self publishers for a long time. There are two ways to make a book free:

KDP Select

You can make a book free by joining KDP Select, the Amazon program. This is the easiest way to get a free book, but it has a nasty downside: when you join Select, you are locked in for 3 months to a contract that requires exclusivity on that title. This means that by putting a book in Select, you are promising Amazon you won't upload it anywhere else. This might not be a big deal if you are a fast writer and put out multiple stories a week, but if you're slower, then this can be dangerous. You won't make any money on Barnes and Noble, Kobo, or Smashwords while in Select, which means you'll be relying solely on money from Amazon for that book. If you're not making much money on those other sites, this might be worth it. I, on the other hand, make as much money on Barnes and Noble as I do on Amazon. I do have a few books in Select because I write fast, but most of my catalog is up on all sites.

While in Select you get 5 days every 3 months in which you can put your book free. People who know better than I, have told me that the best thing to do is to have your books free in 2 day chunks. You can space these out however you like. Amazon Prime members can borrow books that are in KDP select, but you still get paid when your book is borrowed. The money you'll make on a borrowed book is dependent on the Select borrowing "Global Fund". As a rule of thumb, you'll usually make around 2 dollars for every book borrowed.

Price Matching

The other way to make your books free is to have Amazon price match a Barnes and Noble or Kobo price. Via Smashwords you can set your book to free, and that free price will eventually be pushed to Barnes and Noble. You can also set it to free on Kobo. Then, once it's free on those sites, you go to the book page on Amazon, and click on "Tell us about a lower price".

The best thing to do is to have other people, who you're comfortable knowing your pen name, also click the 'lower price' link. The more people who tell Amazon about a lower price, the more likely it is to be price matched in a timely fashion.

This way of price matching can be preferable to some for a few reasons. First of all, obviously, price matching doesn't require you to be exclusive. You get to keep your books up on all of your distributors and still get the kick from having a book free. Secondly, you can have the book be free for as long as you want! You can have it be free for the rest of the copyright's life if you'd like, and it'll always be there to catch the eye of a new reader.

One issue with this is that Amazon might write you an email about it, expressing their displeasure over the issue. They have told multiple people that price matching is acceptable, but they still don't necessarily approve of it. If they do write you a nasty email, don't let it upset you too much. I have not heard a single story of anyone having their account suspended over price matching.

Another issue is that it can be a pain in the neck to have the price put back to normal. You have to wait for the other sites to all have the normal price again, then email Amazon asking for the price match to be removed. This can take a month or longer.

Weigh the pros and cons of each of these options before choosing one!

Giveaways

Another good way to get new readers is to run giveaways. Whether you're giving away your books or an Amazon gift card, you can use Rafflecopter (http://www.rafflecopter.com/) to set them up.

Rafflecopter allows you to have any prize you like, and the best thing is you can make certain things mandatory. You can make it mandatory for people to tweet about your giveaway in order to enter, thereby increasing the number of people who are watching your giveaway. You can make it so they can tweet multiple times a day, too. I've gained many new readers and mailing list subscribers thanks to giveaways.

Some things you might consider giving away:

Amazon gift cards

E-books
Physical books
Sex toys

Each of these things will target different kinds of people. Giving away your own books is really the best way to turn a giveaway entrant into a returning fan, since they'll most likely be entering only if they're interested in your work.

Amazon's Adult Filter

Something has been changing in the Amazon marketplace for a few months now, and many authors are in a little bit of a panic:

What's happening is Amazon is unevenly applying new filters to the erotic fiction being put out, based on keywords in the titles rather than what category they're in. What this means is that if you're not searching correctly, you won't find the erotica you want anymore.

If you're searching on a Kindle, this doesn't seem to apply to you, but if you're on a computer searching through the Amazon store you'll have to take a different approach to find the hot erotica you want to read:
Choose either "Books" or "Kindle Store" to find the erotica you're looking for. Searching through "All" will not give you the same results.

Go to Amazon.com

Next to the search bar, where it says "All", click that and scroll down until you find either "Books" or "Kindle Store" like in the image to the side.

You can now search for the erotica you're looking for.

Please let other erotica authors and readers know about these changes, because the filter will affect almost all authors of smut in the long run. If you're an author and you'd like to know if your stories are filtered, simply search for your pen name on Sales Rank Express. If it's filtered, the word ADULT in bright red letters will be next to your book's title.

Forgotten Sex Toys (Anal Play, BDSM, Dildo Erotica) — **Kindle eBook** — ADULT
Dalia Daudelin | Midnight Climax | 2013-04-07

I hope this post helped! Remember to pass this along to other readers and authors!

CHAPTER FOUR
Fetishes

Fetishes and Why You Care

The pornography industry is based around arousal. Pornographic video can do it with the woman's breasts, butt, face, the guy's physique, face, cock, whatever. It's why the "amateur" porn movement was able to get as big as it is right now—you don't need a story. You don't need to know anything at all about these people, heck you don't really even need to know that the sex makes them feel good. You just need quality visual stimulation.

Erotica isn't that easy. There are people out there who are absolutely gifted. People who can write sex scenes that get me off without ever touching a fetish I'm into. (More than once, I have read a story and then said to myself, 'Good lord, am I into cuckolding now?') With that said, it's uncommon. I've been a fairly decent writer since middle school and I'm nowhere near good enough to evoke the kind of arousal it takes to write something really great without having a specific target audience. Some of my reviewers would even have me believe that knowing my target audience, I'm not evoking the kind of imagery they'd like—enough others disagree that I get by!

There are a wide variety of popular fetishes, and all of them are going to have a major effect on how you write. I'll go into more detail in the bulk of this chapter, but for example:

You have a sex scene between your heroine and her lover. Typically, there's a lot of mechanical in-and-out, of course, but now it's impregnation erotica. Now the threat of impregnation—it is always a threat, never a goal, on the part of at least one character—is constantly looming. No longer is it "You like that?" Now it is "You said you were on the pill, right?"

Fetishes allow us to both define, in advance, how we're going to be writing to a degree, to work within a framework.

However, that's only our use as a writer. There's a much more important role here, for the reader. Readers have many places where they can get their erotic fiction, and not all of them cost money. Fundamentally, you're asking them to give you their money, and of course they aren't going to do it for something they don't understand. Now, your blurb (Chapter 3) is going to do a lot of work toward selling your story, but to get that initial click you've got to have a strong cover, strong title, and strong tagging (above)—all of these are defined by the fetishes you're targeting.

Fetish targeting allows the writer and the reader to communicate in shorthand about what is going to be occurring in the story.

A (pseudo-)incest story is going to be romantic, in some sense, about exploring sexual boundaries. I don't need to tag it as "romance" or "first time," most of the time, because those things are part of the much bigger package of "incest."

On the other hand, if you had a story about cuckolding, having a virginal female is highly unusual. You'd absolutely have to tag it or mention it in the blurb, because that's not part of the accepted meaning of cuckolding.

That's why I hope you'll understand when I claim that fetish selection is absolutely the most important part of writing an erotic story of any kind. Many of my stories began with a discussion between my fiancé and I, where I say that I'm between ideas and he says 'Just write lactation.' The idea doesn't have to go further than that before I start writing the sex scene—at that point, I already know what the smut needs, and the story will grow out of that fairly organically.

Taboo

Before I get to specifics, though, I should really discuss where all of this fetish talk comes from. Are people dirty cretins who are incapable of enjoying regular old sex? Of course not!

The thing is, as odd as it is to say in the porn industry, you're intellectually stimulating people, not visually or physically—though I'd say that physical stimulation might not be called pornography anymore!—and as a result you have to have something that appeals to the mind.

Again, there's a perfectly valid point to be made that for those of us who are exemplary, talent can make someone describing, say, a breast into something arousing for a person. But that's not me, and I hope you won't take it as rude of me to say that it's probably not you, either.

Intellectual arousal, sexual arousal that comes from thinking about stuff, is overwhelmingly from the idea of **taboo**. It's by far the most common sexual fetish, but it's also the hardest to pin down (hence the reason we have the long section on fetishes—these are all sub-categories of 'taboo.'

People enjoy the idea of doing something they're not supposed to do. I always referred to it in myself as a "bad idea fetish." It's this nameless desire to do something you know you'll regret for a thrill.

Of course, the thrill comes from the risk of consequence. And that's what you need to stress, to varying degrees, no matter what you're writing.

Incest is a fetish about love, fundamentally. In most cases, it's about such a powerful love that it overcomes the social taboo attached. On the other hand, the consequence is constantly niggling at the gate—will the parents find out that our heroine's been fooling around with her stepbrother? Will they be forced apart by circumstance? However, that's just one driving force, and the fact is that the love and lust should overcome, and should be the primary focus. The consequence is just a cherry on top.

Compare to Impregnation, or Exhibitionism: literally fetishes of consequence. The thrill here, the sexual tension and subsequent release, all comes from the constant threat of this lasting consequence (a baby and arrest, respectively). Any romance is secondary, a peculiarity of your individual story rather than a core element of the sub-genre.

Reversal

Additionally, however, you can't have predictability AND intellectual stimulation. There should always be a question in the reader's mind, 'is everything going to go the way I expect it to?'

Let's take a short break from erotica here to look at genre

fiction in general, in particular (considering our audience) the romance novel. The current King of Romance is, in my mind, Nicholas Sparks. And all of his novels follow, to a degree, a pattern: the traditional Romance pattern, in truth.

Central to the formula for Romance is the constant attack on the relationship. In *The Notebook*, for instance, you have the heroine's mother, the heroine's fiancé, her entire social place opposes her relationship with the hero. Everything tells us that these two people should not be together, and because we want them to be, as a result of good storytelling, these things come together to create conflict and tension.

Until almost the end of the story, *The Notebook* creates an excellent air of uncertainty, almost of doom. I'm not asking that of you, I'm just asking that you have some tension. Just because we're not planning on writing international bestsellers here, we don't want to write off tension as a storytelling tool. In fact, realistically, that's how sexual pleasure works, too. Sexual enjoyment is all about building up tension and then releasing it (or, in some circles, not releasing it, but that's neither here nor there).

To bring the discussion back to erotica into focus, consider my story *Stepdaddy, Send Me to Paris*. Sissy is the pen name I use for pseudo-incest. The central fetish is actually closer to Billionaire stories, and in that context it's fairly standard. The story revolves around a girl who is presented with two choices—go on her dream vacation and sleep with her stepfather, or keep her purity and, well, *not*.

Of course, it also borders on Dubious Consent—it's a lot of fetishes to be perfectly honest, but the entire time there's the very real question of whether or not this is going to cause real irreparable harm to her mother's relationship, whether or not she'll go through with it, if it's almost rape or if it's something she's at least somewhat enjoying. This uncertainty continues well into the steamy bits, and I daresay it doesn't suffer for it.

The point I'm trying to make here is this: For every single rule I state in this chapter, understand that the exact opposite outcome is equally valid, equally effective. The primary thing to keep in mind is that all the fetishes we're going to be discussing are focused on particular elements. If you focus on them, you don't have to go the way I recommend. You'd probably do well not to always do the most expected thing. Just keep in mind: your readers expect you to deal with specific issues in your material. As long as you deliver on your promises, most people will be happy.
Brother/sister incest, I'll get to below, is built on the relationship that develops over the years and years of knowing each other, and being around each other as sexuality is still growing and changing. But on the other hand, siblings from a broken home, who are distant, but bridge that gap through sexuality is equally fitting for the genre.

Billionaire

Billionaire stories are a relatively new fetish, in that like so many of the others, this has a long-standing basis but we can pinpoint specifically when it became a big seller: It became a big seller in the wake of *Fifty Shades of Grey*. There's not much else to it. In its purest form you want to deliver the same kind of sex that *Fifty Shades* delivered. However, a similar power dynamic works about as well.
The formula is also fairly set. The viewpoint character is

almost always a woman: she needs money so she finds a billionaire who wants sex in exchange. There are exceptions, of course, as with everything.

Only, it's never 'vanilla' sex. It's always pushing the bounds of what the heroine is really comfortable with. If she's a virgin, it might just be giving up her virginity, but more commonly this mixes with BDSM and rape themes. It's important to keep in mind that where BDSM is all about unspoken boundaries and trust, this is the opposite, without becoming really unpleasant like rape fantasies often do—I'll get into those later.

Billionaire fantasies are about allowing lines to be crossed, about mistrust and yet, possibly, love in spite of that. It's pretty much a great excuse to portray unhealthy relationships, and that's something you have to understand if you're going to write billionaire erotica. However, in the wake of *Twilight* and subsequently *Fifty Shades*, readers often want unhealthy relationships in their stories. So try not to rub in their face that it's unhealthy, just describe the relationship in its codependent glory without comment.

The other way this goes, which is perhaps less offensive in terms of the gender roles and stereotypes, is that the woman/ viewpoint character decides to use the tool at her disposal, namely sexual desire, to get something she wants. There's no air of blackmail, of the girl not truly being in a position to say 'no' here—she chose this.

In this case, it's important to realize that your heroine can be easily interpreted as a gold-digger: that's because she is. There's no shame in it, but trying to humanize her is going to make your story more confused, and it's not going to work in the long run anyways. Instead, you need to make it clear that your heroine is doing something she does not consider a moral issue.

Billionaire is one of the best-selling subgenres, and at the same time one of the easiest to write, since the characters are essentially stock pieces who need only minimal back-story or development. This is a wonderful genre for beginning writers, or writers who want to be able to focus largely on the sexual aspect, without needing to get too much into the psychology of the sex act that's occurring, which is central to almost every other fetish (with the possible exception of the more physical fetishes like lactation or urine play).

Uncomfortable Subject Warning

As a courtesy, I'm going to warn you now: The rest of this chapter is going to be discussing a number of fairly uncomfortable and very possibly offensive subjects in very frank terms. I hope that if you're worried about being offended, you'll look through the Table of Contents and decide which sections, if any, you would like to read or skip.

BDSM

BDSM is a very complex subject. In many ways it's 'Alice down the rabbit hole,' and it goes as deep as you want it to go. But there are limits to how much people want to read about BDSM—or at least, I believe that.
Are there people who get piercings to hang from ropes attached to the ceiling using only their skin? Yes. Does that translate well to BDSM-targeted erotica? Not that I know of. Not that I've ever read.

The primary draw of the BDSM genre is actually what the BDSM community proper would call D/s, or Dominance and submission: it's about the power dynamic. In this way, it's a close relative of the Billionaire genre, which is in no small way related to the fact that the Billionaire genre got its biggest kick-start with a BDSM story. However, while Billionaire stories are all about unchecked power, BDSM is about an understanding of where the line is, and trusting someone not to cross the line even while they dance around it.

However, dominance is easiest to demonstrate through BDSM play. As much as it isn't fair to real life, "dominant" can be used as interchangeable with "sadist" and "submissive" can be used to mean "masochist." A blurring of the lines between sexuality and violence is common. Blurred lines between sexuality and non-sexuality are even more blurred.

For example, in a "standard," non-fetish story having the woman's husband ask her to get a beer is a non-event. It's just taking up space. It might even be offensive, depending on the context and the way that the husband phrases it.

In a dominant-submissive relationship, it can be used as a tool to demonstrate the relationship dynamic. She's not doing it because she'd get anyone a beer, because Hey, she's right by the fridge. She's doing it in spite of the fact that he's clearly closer, because it's a test of her loyalty and she wants to pass the test.

It can be tempting to think that gender equality would see the woman being the dominant figure sometimes—perhaps even often.

I cannot recommend this unless you're writing lesbian porn,

because I cannot in good conscience recommend writing from a male perspective for a male-oriented fetish (which female dominance is) with a primarily female audience, and I cannot recommend writing from the perspective of the Dom regardless of gender.

My fiancé is a sadist—the sex is generally normal, but it comes out on occasion. The one thing that he was very clear to me about, when we discussed this for the sake of my work, is that it's not exactly a sexual pleasure. It's a trade of sexual satisfaction for emotional or intellectual stimulation.
It can be portrayed in written form. I've done it, in *Fifty Shades Reversed*. The problem is that it became clear fairly early in the sex scene that it wasn't erotic. It was about a power trip, a feeling of having control and having someone in your power. There was no way that I could find to make that erotic for someone who wasn't already familiar with the feeling, who wasn't already a sadist.
On the other hand, portraying submission as erotic is relatively trivial. Submission is inherently built around demonstrations of love, and trying to portray the enjoyment of pain is a difficult task made easier by explaining it in part as involving understanding your partner.
There should always be communication between lovers, and in BDSM relationships this is even more true—in erotica, however, BDSM should almost be mind-reading. Unspoken understandings abound.

For this reason, BDSM is often about the romantic elements inherent in the dominant-submissive relationship. However, there are multiple alternative directions to take the portrayal that can maintain an erotic tone without alienating readers who don't partake in BDSM play themselves.

The biggest emotion involved in nearly all forms of BDSM is a loss of control. People who have experienced this in a controlled sexual setting often attest to how arousing the experience is, and how liberating. To many people, especially women, sexuality is at best thin ice, and they worry that enjoying or even pursuing sexual experiences makes them "dirty" or "slutty."

The loss of control in even very light bondage play allows this weight to be lifted from their shoulders. Though we are in the business of pornography, there is absolutely no reason not to take advantage of these sorts of situations and how relatable they are to the average reader.

Related to all of this is the idea of service to the master or dominant, particularly in stories from the perspective of the submissive. This is a fairly complex part of BDSM psychology, but in short you can take it as a sign of devotion to a dominant that the submissive can take part in, as well as a sign of submission. It's a very important part of the relationship dynamic, and shouldn't be ignored.

On the other hand, there's "bratty" submissives, who are disobedient, often as a way to elicit discipline from their dominant. That can translate very well into your erotica, as well.

DubCon/Rape

Following from the loss-of-control ideas in bondage, the entire rape fetish is based around that ideal. In male-oriented pornography, there is a strong air of humiliation, even as the man is dehumanized as essentially meat.

In erotica, on the other hand, as with almost everything else, the focus is squarely on the emotional experience. Fear is a powerful aphrodisiac and makes most experiences more pointed, more "present." At the same time, the victim can't control the situation—much more than in BDSM stories. In reality, if a BDSM situation gets out of hand it can be stopped, and many people in the back of their minds realize this even in fantasy, so it feels like even still control's not absolutely gone. Enter the rape fantasy, which absolutely removes any amount of control from the victim. Ultimately, it's about power dynamics, analogous to billionaire stories or BDSM. Rape is a very touchy subject for a lot of people (which, incidentally, is why we've cordoned it off: in case you as a writer aren't comfortable with it!) and there's a lot of dancing around the issue with most people. There are almost never lasting consequences for the victim, almost always it's an event that was unforeseen and unforeseeable. Yet, at the same time, almost every time it was a stranger—essentially, the rape fantasy is based around the Ted Bundy myth of a stranger who rapes at random (though rarely do the victims die at the end).

It's much, much more important that you portray the victim. Historically, rape was often used as a tool, rather than as an interpersonal attack which is more common today--so you might be able to make an argument for a historical story built around rape-as-marriage, but otherwise the rape fantasy is a stronger form of the power trip that colors portrayals of the dominant in a BDSM story. In my opinion, there is no way to make a violent rape into an erotic experience. I cannot say in any sort of stronger words: do not make an attempt to do anything of the sort, it will not succeed and you risk alienating some portion of your audience in trying.

However, it's not entirely fair to spend all this time on the subject of rape. There are two reasons that the word "dubious consent" is used. First, because out-and-out rape is not allowed on Amazon, so it's generally preferred to make it 'maybe rape' where the girl says no, the guy takes what he wants, and then the girl decides she likes it after all. Second, though, is because it's actually an umbrella term for other consent-based kinks like reluctance or coercion.

Reluctance should come in to play in almost all of the stories involving Billionaires. The psychology of why reluctance is erotic is a little bit challenging, so I won't try to explain it. Just know that the fetish relies on a character who would rather not have sex, but isn't exactly saying no, either. Coercion is similar, but involves a certain amount of mind games so in some ways it's closer to 'rape' than it is to 'reluctance.'
A common storyline in reluctance-based or coercion-based erotica is where the person wants something—as simple as a ride home or as big as a job, and the person in power offers it to them at the expense of sex. Keep in mind when you're writing that the viewpoint should be uncertain of how far they're willing to go, but eventually cave in.

Incest
Incest is a tricky topic to discuss in open terms. Most people,

the vast majority in my experience, are at least somewhat intrigued by incest as a pornographic experience, whether or not they'll admit it to someone else.

If you try to discuss the idea of incest with someone as a real-world occurrence, they're often upset and a little disturbed by it. But the moment it becomes a fantasy, they're all over it. This is a theme that's going to occur again a few times, especially rape. So I want to stress this early on: None of these fetishes have much to do with the real-world equivalent. In real life, incest is almost always between generational gaps and almost always coercive. That's why "Rape and Incest" are used as a pair so often: Incest is very often a matter of Uncle Creepy telling Little Susan that she shouldn't tell her parents about their games, and it's ok because it's just for play, etc. Creepy sex, not steamy hot erotic sex. That's not what we're talking about, thankfully.

However, due to the incredibly taboo, highly illegal nature of incest as both a fetish and a real occurrence, Amazon will not let you sell porn involving actual incest. For this reason, the field is referred to as "pseudo-incest," and generally involves step-siblings, step-parents, etc. As long as it is absolutely clear that there is no blood relation, you're fine.
Understand that there are interesting things you can do with this relationship, which differentiate step-siblings from actual siblings in terms of the emotional dynamic. For example, a common story in the world of Japanese porn comics, where incest is only somewhat taboo, is that a pair was lovers and then their parents marry, putting them into the unenviable position of being step-siblings and making a non-incestuous

relationship into a pseudo-incestuous one.

That, too, is not generally what we're going to be discussing. Most of the time, when you hear someone refer to pseudo-incest, what they mean is "incest, but without a blood relation, because I don't want to get my entire library taken down."

So with that in mind, when I discuss the subject, I'm going to skip the "step" nomenclature, since it just takes up space, and is there as a technicality in most cases. Understand that when you're writing, all of this material applies, but they cannot be related by blood.

Siblings

One of the big three relationships; of them, sibling relationships are by far the most vanilla. There are certain expectations about the relationship between siblings, which allow the reader and the writer to work with pre-existing understandings.

Think of it, to a degree, as being less rigorous fan-fiction. You don't need to establish with your reader in any direct way that these two are very close, or that they have a history together. It's implied by their sibling relationship.

At the same time, at its purest, this is a pairing that works at a youngish age, around the time that people start experimenting with their sexuality, between 14 and 17. Those people are strictly, 100% off limits to write about as a pornographer who wants to sell their material. That's absolutely illegal; nobody will allow you to sell that material. Most places that will even allow you to post it on their servers try to wash their hands of responsibility to your content, because all it would take is one too many complaints and their server is down for child pornography.

So, again, we have to write stories with the details changed a bit, because the themes have nothing to do with child pornography and everything to do with accessible emotions that everyone goes through. So we call them 18 and pretend they're a very naive 18.

Essentially, you want to create a relationship between the two that is built around the idea of safety and comfort. I have seen very good stories break this rule, but never a good one that only bent it. Either you have an environment of absolute distrust, or an environment of trust. There's no environment of apathy.

The fetish here is, as I said, built around exploring sexuality. It's almost always the first time for one or both of the participants. The taboo nature of what they're about to do is a constant problem that plagues the lovers and clouds their minds with doubt.

Longer stories will often have repeated attempts to stop seeing each other because 'it's too dangerous,' or because of an external threat of being exposed.

The overall theme here is that their love—for it is love, even when it's clouded by lust—overcomes their fears and society's rules. Often, I daresay most of the time, these have a male point of view, which is a relative rarity in the erotica world. Because most consumers of erotica are women, it's generally considered less profitable. However, there are plenty of exceptions to the rule, so don't take it as gospel.

As a special aside, there are also cousin relationships.

These are much less common, outside the top 3, but contain essentially the same relationship dynamic as siblings, with the added twist of being somewhat less taboo (though still very much so) and being more 'exotic,' as opposed to someone who you see every day. They function as a sort-of middle ground between the deeply incestuous sibling relationship, and a more normal "first time" story.

DADDY-DAUGHTER

The parent-child relationships are split here, because they're very, very different. In both cases, they're dominated by the woman's point of view, and in both cases they involve a degree of power dynamic (which we've discussed in the Billionaire and BDSM sections), but that's essentially where the similarities stop.

In the case of a father-daughter relationship, a great deal of care has to be taken to avoid unwanted implication of the father being "creepy." It's a very easy trap to fall into if you're not careful.
The dynamic here is based around the daughter looking up to her father. Again, as with all incest, there is a degree of fudging ages here, as the most powerful incest stories take place when the younger participant is first exploring their sexuality. The daughter is noticing men, and yet she can't help but notice that her father seems so perfect.
The mother is almost always out of the picture, and the father is lonely and overworked. The daughter wants to comfort him, and at the same time she wants to deal with the emotions bottled up inside her.

On the other hand, you can write a very convincing alternative—one which falls straight into the trap of potentially creepy father figures, as it happens—where the father uses his position of prestige in the family (again, almost always with the mother out of the picture) to get what he wants, which is sexual release. Again, however, we have themes of the father being bottled up.

MOTHER-SON

This is perhaps the least common of the three, roughly as common as cousin-incest. It is also somewhat unusual in that the father is still in the picture as often as not, which adds a degree of breaking the family unit that is uncommon to incest fantasies.

There are a few ways to tell this story. The first and most common is that the son is attracted to the mother, and she feels obligated to reciprocate his feelings. Often, she will be reluctant to have any sort of relationship, and there's a great deal of hand wringing and hesitation before moving the sexual element further.

Rarely is there any romantic attachment here; the other two contain a lot of emotional baggage, of romantic love, while this entire range is familial love expressed through sexuality. Another common story, particularly in Japan (where helicopter parenting is a much bigger problem than in the west) is that the mother wants to see that her son is prepared for the outside world. A common non-incest variant on this story is that a boy is dating a girl, and the girl's mother wants to ensure he is sexually capable enough for her daughter.

Other relationships are almost always either a milder form of one of these core relationships, or a "hook" for a BDSM/DubCon story, where instead of coming up with some convoluted reason that the girl is forced to strip, her grandfather's writing his will etc. The latter almost never have a romantic attachment, and almost never need to avoid the "trap" of creepy men: indeed, that's the entire plan.

Other

There are other fetishes. Most of them are very niche, but there's no reason not to diversify your library.

WATERSPORTS

Urine-play is perhaps one of the easiest fetishes for authors to understand, and one of the hardest fetishes for people to grasp if they're not personally into it.

See, people in real life almost never have urine-play in their sex. But in the world of writing, it's very common that if a story has come out a little bland, then adding a few very taboo fetishes will make it more appealing to the hardcore crowd. Watersports is one of the favorite options for this, since it requires almost no lead-in or storyline explanation, while adding an incestuous relationship or BDSM will affect the tone of the story.

With that said, the primary thing to keep in mind is that when you're peeing after you've held it for a very long time, the feeling's similar to an orgasm, and when you're talking about watersports, it's got a very pure focus on the actions involved, so it's all about describing that action rather than trying to make it fit into a good story.

CUCKOLDING

Cuckolding is an incredibly popular fetish as part of the next section, impregnation, but also in its own right. Centrally, the idea is that a woman is cheating on the man, but the man is aroused by the idea of it. That differentiates it from standard cheating, where the thrill is of something different from the 'norm' and the risk of doing something immoral.
Cuckolding is all about the woman's actions, but oddly it's about the man's desires, and that's what's important. Keep the focus there and you should be okay.

IMPREGNATION

This fetish is based entirely around unsafe sex. There are generally three ways this goes.
First are "true stories," which are unusually kinky but not outside the realm of possibility. Almost never true, but the goal is to make it seem very plausible.
Second are, what I would call, "malicious" impregnations: one partner tricks the other into having unsafe sex, without their knowledge or really their consent. This is DubCon in the strictest sense, but rarely carries the heavy violent or coercive tones of rape fantasies. This is more rape-by-deception. This can go either way; women generally sabotage condoms or hold men inside through some method. Men fail to pull out, or trick women into believing they are wearing a condom when they're not. Of course, there are other options, but those are the most common.

Third are 'fetish' impregnations. There's impregnation occurring, and the general rules of the fetish apply, but a greater focus is on the fetish—cuckolding, public sex, etc. It varies widely, dependent upon the 'main' fetish.

Generally, the major theme of impregnation stories is the risk, and in turn the thrill of taking that risk. A common shortcut to focus on this is the word "potent." Everything comes back around to the fact that sperm = babies, and there's going to be sperm where babies are made.

PARANORMAL

If Billionaire is popular because of *Fifty Shades*, this is the culmination of *Twilight*. This is often the first stepping stone women have into the world of erotica, because it's such a short leap from young adult paranormal romance to "grown up" paranormal romance, which at the very least tinges on erotica (for example, Anne Rice). A heavier focus on the romance, and a desire to see the romance play out to its finale among girls who already know plenty about sexuality, leads straight into paranormal erotica.

This can take many forms, and all of them are going to focus somewhat on trying to get the lore right. I'm not going to discuss it here, but suffice it to say that if you're going to discuss vampires, know how vampires are supposed to work. There's a lot of wiggle room, but it's absolutely never wise to make a change to established lore that readers are already going to know about without a good reason.

A possible exception exists in the world of Vampires, since Twilight tore down so many barriers in that area. However,

*there's no good reason to take a third option—feel free
to co-opt Twilightesque vampires, as long as they're not
the Cullens, but don't write Vampires as zombies—that's
stretching things just as much as if you wrote a Golem love
story where Golems are treated as weak saps.*

LACTATION

This goes hand-in-hand with impregnation in some ways—
namely, that impregnation gets you here in the first place.
It carries a lot of baggage regarding motherhood and it's
important not to ignore that. However, this is an odd fetish in
that like urine play, it's got very little to do with an emotional
connection and relationship being played out through the sex,
and almost everything to do with describing an erotic act. This
is best played out in a romantic setting, or another emotional
frame provided by a more structured fetish like pseudo-incest
or billionaire.

CHAPTER FIVE
Cover Design

Elements of Cover Design

There are a number of elements that make up a professional-level cover; it's not any single skill, and everyone is going to be better at some parts than others. My fiancé and I work on covers together, one of our compromises in our business, and I'd say that we both have things we're better at. I've got his input here, so hopefully nothing will be left out.

Firstly, you're almost certainly going to be using stock images, rather than hiring your own models, photographing your own shots, and so on. That's so far beyond the scope of this manual, we're not even going to get into it. That's an entire career on its own and it deserves more space than we've got here.

Selecting good stock is a skill, but it's not an absolute necessity. We've kicked out some very good covers with very lackluster stock photos, and it's all about how you use them. To re-purpose an old adage, 'it's not the size of the boat, it's the motion of the ocean.' It can't be more true than in this case. With that said, you want a certain amount of sexual energy in your stock photos, if you can get it, without being too racy to get past content filters.

Some of our more tame covers have had attractive people in non-sexual situations, and after everything was said and done, we changed to a more sexually charged image for the second edition in almost every case. That hasn't stopped us from continuing to use tame covers, of course, but it's a lesson we've learned that being tame should be a conscious choice.

On the other hand, it's worth noting that there are limits, both hard limits by distributors and limits of good taste. For example, Amazon will not allow nudity. No matter how good the image is, if it's got a bared breast you need to cover it up somehow because otherwise Amazon's not going to allow that cover.

It's possible that you may find a cover that is within Amazon's limitations of what is technically allowable, but inappropriate. A woman sucking on a hot dog held at waist height by an attractive man would be inappropriate for almost anything, for example. It's just too direct, too explicit, too much. So there is a point where you're not tame *enough*, as well.

Then there's framing. Mostly when people talk about this in the context of photography and design, they mean "putting the good bits in the right spots," but it also means putting things in a way that later steps are going to make good sense.

For example, it might seem to make sense to have a bright white line going vertically through your cover. That said, it's going to make text placement a nightmare and you will probably regret it. I'll be discussing how and where this all fits later.

Once you've got your image selected, cropped to size (and shape), and any edits that need to be made are finished, you get to the stage where your brand can be properly established: fonts.

This is a fairly complicated subject (the majority of book design is font work in one way or another) and I can only give you the beginning steps. With that said, you should be able to take what I will discuss and use your own judgment to establish a fairly solid sense of style.

Putting all these things together, you can try to form a framework of how your design should look, both on a case-by-case basis and as a brand for the day when people actually look for you by name. You can do this through two things: layout and color palette selection. There are certain basic rules you're going to want to follow, but trying to follow them in a consistent way can help to make your library look like it "fits" together—look at any mass printing of a series of novels, and you'll see consistent design. That's what you want to create for yourself.

Stock Photos

There are 3 different kinds of stock you want to look for: Photos with sexy women, photos with sexy men, and photos with sexy couples.

Stock of Women

For photos of sexy women, it's helpful to search for the following keywords:

Sexy lady
Erotic lady
Sexy fashion
Fashion
Hand cuffs
Bondage
Underwear
Bathing suit

Of course there are other keywords that you can try, which you'll figure out. These keywords will bring up hundreds of images on the various stock websites.

Stock of Men

Photos of sexy men are much harder to find. If you find a good model that you like, I recommend getting all of his images and then looking through the portfolio of the photographer he works with. You might find more.

The following keywords will help you find sexy men:

Sexy man
Business man
Man in suit
Muscles

Stock of Couples

Stock of couples shouldn't be too hard to find. As with

stock of men, it's helpful to look through the portfolios of photographers that you like. Not all of their photos will show up in searches since they may be using weird keywords.

If you're looking for gay or lesbian couples, well, good luck. They're not easy to find. Eroticstockphotos.com has a selection of gay and lesbian couples that is growing rapidly, and probably has the best selection you'll find anywhere.

The following keywords will help you find photos of couples:

Date
Sexy date
Sex
Sexy couple

Examples

When looking at these images, you want to find photos that don't come off as if they belong in a fashion catalog. You also want photos that are longer vertically than horizontally. You're looking for scantily clad women, women showing off cleavage, and women in suggestive poses.

This photo is a good example of stock that would be perfect for a cover. It conveys a story. This cover would be perfect for a billionaire story, since the man is clearly wearing a suit. The billionaire should probably tie the female protagonist up in the story, or use some other form of bondage as well.

Aside from conveying the story, it also has the benefit of being sexy, but still beautiful. It's not too sexy, so it won't likely get your book filtered by Amazon. It's vertical, making it easy to convert into a cover. All of these things make this a perfect stock photo choice.

This stock photo would be perfect for an erotic romance or romance, probably something longer than a simple short. It would obviously need to be rotated so that it's vertical, but is otherwise a good choice. There is a chance, though, that

Apple's iTunes bookstore won't accept the cover, as they don't seem to like black and white covers. It may help to color her lips red or add color to the background in order to avoid that issue. A colored font would also more than likely be a good choice.

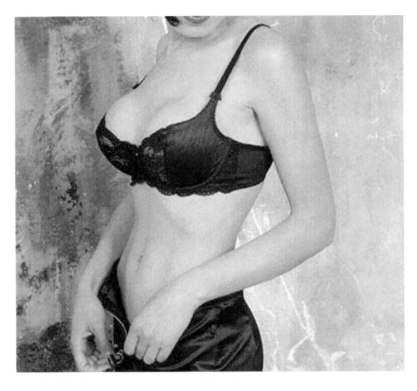

This photo would be great for a simple erotic short. It doesn't convey much story, but the emphasis on her breasts make this especially suited for a lactation short. You will, however, want to crop the image so that it's 6x9 instead of square. Keep in mind, however, the change in color. Light fonts don't work well on light backgrounds, and dark fonts don't work well on dark backgrounds. So try to be conscious when cropping to make a space where you can fit your title.

This image, however, is a bad choice. It conveys a story that makes it great for a vampire erotica or erotic romance, but since it is longer horizontally it poses many challenges. There is no good way to crop this. In order to make it work, you'd have to extend the background upwards, which requires more technical knowledge than a beginner will have. Unless you are skilled in a photo editing programming, skip images like this.

And as a last note, remember: Images are property. People own those photos, and many expect to make money from them. If the photographer says that the image is free for any use, then you can use it without paying them—always attribute. If you somehow found a way to use stock photos without paying their license fees, or something of that nature, you are depriving that photographer of the money they earned. It's not fair to them, and you shouldn't do it.

Fonting

I'd like to just hop right in here, but there are a few things I should discuss first. Primarily, I want to define a few very basic concepts in fonts, so that you can use your own judgment in what works for any given story. This is a big subject (so many of the subjects we're dealing with are!) but I'll try to give a primer here.

There are two basic "types" of font: Serif and Sans-Serif ("without Serif"). Basically, a "serif" is the little tag on some letters, especially lower case. At its most basic, it helps to differentiate some letters, symbols, and characters. Allow me to illustrate what I mean.

Look at the average printed handwriting, and you'll find that without any serifs or distinguishing marks, the capital "I", the lower-case "L" and the numeral "1" look identical: one vertical mark of capital height. There are other marks that can be difficult to distinguish, such as the letter "O" and the numeral "0", or the lower-case "T" made without a bent vertical and the "+" sign.

That's why for most people, when making a printed capital "I," will mark it with horizontal bits at top and bottom. Those are serifs. The marker on the top-left of the "1" is also a serif, though it is so commonly used that it is often found in sans-serif fonts.

Of course, there are things in between, fonts where only the most important serifs are used (semi-sans), or where some of the less-important serifs are removed (semi-serif).

Most people regard Sans-Serif as being easier to read, particularly from a distance or in small print, while Serif fonts are more pleasing to the eye. Think of the difference between poetry and a quick-start guide, essentially.
For this reason, in my covers, where my name is printed relatively small, and my tags smaller still, we use a Semi-Sans or Sans-Serif font. On the other hand, for the title font, most of our fonts have Serifs.

For titling in particular, hand-written and calligraphic fonts are also common. While they can be expressed in terms of serifed and sans-serif, it's not common to do so.
Hand-written fonts have their use, but those uses are very specific. In general, don't use handwriting fonts. Their use should be a conscious choice to break the rules, rather than considered a valid option.

There are generally two types of calligraphic fonts that are appropriate. Copperplate/Spencerian-esque fonts is widely used for romance—the most famous by far is Zapfino, to the point that there are many Zapf replicas and variations floating around. A good free alternative is Champignon. On the other hand, italic fonts are somewhat hard to explain to non-calligraphers because of the use of "italic" to mean "slanted" in general font use. My preferred italic is Trixite No 1 Italic, but Chancery Cursive is an acceptable free alternative. An italic of this kind is widely applicable, but maintains the formality of the more flowing Zapf-like scripts. It can work for something like a billionaire BDSM story in the vein of *Fifty Shades*, but we didn't feel it was appropriate for, say, dildo bike stories such as *A Taboo Ride*'s sub-parts.

Of course, you're not going to want to use the same 4-5 fonts for all your covers. If you want to buy fonts and have the resources to do so, that's going to work wonderfully, and you can access the best fonts in the world. However, there are many very good fonts you can get completely free; DaFont. com is a very good source, as few of their fonts are absolutely unsuitable to any use.

It's important here, however, to keep track of licenses. On DaFont, there is a search function which will allow you to search by license. "Free" or "Public Domain/GPL" are both acceptable for you to use in your covers (as well as interiors for printed work, covered later). Your use is commercial, and certainly not personal use. Anything more restrictive than that, and you're not only breeching ethical boundaries, you're breaking copyright law. I will (and have done so up until now) only suggest fonts that are either non-free or are free for commercial use in this book. In the case of paid fonts, above, I have tried to provide some alternative.

Layout Considerations

It's very easy, initially, to get overwhelmed trying to lay out a cover. The entire thing can seem random, even once you have your font chosen. Therefore, it's important to establish fairly early a few guiding ideas, and move on from there.

In theory, there are infinite placement possibilities, but in practice there are 9 places you can position text. Assuming you follow my sizing guideline of 6x9 at 300dpi (an 1800x2700 image)

With the top left corner at 75, 75;
With the top center at 900, 75;
With the top right corner at 1725, 75;
With the center left at 75, 1350;
With the exact center at 900, 1350;
With the center right at 1725, 1350;
With the bottom left corner at 75, 2625;
With the bottom center at 900, 2625;
With the bottom right corner at 1725, 2625

Like so:

TITLE   TITLE   TITLE

TITLE   TITLE   TITLE

TITLE   TITLE   TITLE

The important idea here is that you're putting a 75 pixel margin inside the image that's not going to be seen in the final result, but outside of which no text should go. Outside of that consideration, we're trying to place things on the points of a 3x3 grid that takes up the entire image (not counting margins). With that in mind, your title text should take up as much space as it can without obstructing the image. As with everything else, it's a balancing act. You want to get as large as possible without ever risking becoming too large. Therefore, err on the side of smaller than necessary. Generally my text is 5.5 inches (1650 px) wide unless there's some other contributing factor—for instance, the cover to *Take Me* has a silhouette that takes up the left side of the image, so I wanted to preserve that silhouette if possible. Therefore, the text took up less space than usual in the interest of that preservation.

Vertical balance is a good goal to have as well. If the title is at the top, then your tags and name should go toward the bottom. However, there have been many cases where the balance is provided by the stock you're using. To reuse an example, the cover of my story *Take Me* has so much going on toward the left that the text is all on the right. There's nothing wrong with that, because I'm balancing the space used by the background as well. Interestingly, I also have the text at 3 o'clock and 4.30 o'clock, which is balanced by the face at 10.30. Compare, for example:

The other consideration is branding. Essentially, you want to keep in mind that similar looking covers, covers that look like they go together, will create a stronger memory of your product in the mind of your readers. You want to try to have as many repetitive elements as possible, so when readers see something that you've done—possibly even when it was someone else using a similar technique, they immediately think of you.

That's branding, and every major company you care to name spends the majority of their advertising budget trying to get it just right because it's the single most important part of forming a reliable group of return customers.

Initially, there should be a few things you want to decide right away, namely the font you want to use when you put your name on the cover, and how you want it sized. This should be consistent throughout your library. This has been the constant between all of us at Midnight Climax, and I've helped with every cover we've done. Each of us have a very typical, very noticeable style for our author name on the cover, and if you've seen it once, you'll recognize it the next time because it's only a minor variation on the theme.

This should also apply to the title font, but only in a series. You can afford to use similar layouts, similar font styles, etc in stories that are in the same series, or stories that are basically similar (two BDSM stories, for example) but it begins to strain credulity when your brutal BDSM font is used for a romantic incest story.

Coloring Considerations

Coloring is incredibly complicated. Compared to most subjects here, which are all fairly complicated, this is by far the most complicated. However, it's also a lot of complicated stuff that you only sort-of need.

The entire idea of color selection is trying to balance colors. There is a massive world of color theory and it all has to do with trying to figure out some way to achieve balance that isn't the same as the way they were doing it before.

There are, generally, two ways to achieve "balance." You learned the basics of both of them in even the most basic art class: Value (or dark-vs-light) and the color wheel.

VALUE

Basically, when dealing with starkly dark and light colors, be aware of the balance. Perfect "balance" would be symmetrical. However, perfect lack of balance is also considered balanced, for example if you had the left half black and the right half white. It isn't perfectly symmetrical, but it's a clear asymmetry, and it's really got a mirrored quality. On the other hand, if the left half were white, and the right half were zebra-striped, then it would look odd, because now it's not a contrasted balance that makes sense.

Initially, you want to look at the image you've selected, and try to figure out how the value balances. Most photographers are going to have a very good understanding of balance and composition, better than you can expect to get from a book that is realistically more about writing and marketing than artistic composition. The balance should be fairly easy to grasp; perhaps it will be centered around a figure, perhaps it will be split vertically or horizontally in some way (for example, a profile-view of a head on the left side of the image, against a white backdrop). There's a lot of possible variation, but it should be immediately obvious.

Then you can try to figure out how your font can work. If there is sufficient space then you're going to want to try to work within the territory of that balance, and let the stock speak for itself. Most of the time, though, it won't be ideal. Instead, you're going to need to figure out a way to bridge separate parts of the image with your text, and almost always you will do so by having the text span the whole image.

COLOR

Secondly, there are color balances. You don't want to use too many colors in the image—more than 4 completely different colors and things begin to get confusing. Of course, multiple similar shades of red can all be fairly called "red." So you really want no more than 4 "ideas" of colors, if that makes sense.

There's complementary colors, which is the typical choice for a two-color composition. Red and green, blue and orange, yellow and purple, etc. These are opposites on the color wheel. There are not many other options for a two-color composition. These tend to be very glaring, and you'll want to use colors with low saturation when you choose to do this to minimize the clashing effect.

CHAPTER SIX
Formatting

Manual vs Automatic Formatting

There are three ways to get your files formatted properly for digital distribution.

First, you can submit a .doc file with your story. On the opposite end of the spectrum, you can convert your story to .mobi and .epub files yourself. In between, you can use a tool to convert for you.

The specific details of how to hand-make your eBook files are beyond the scope of this document—it's discussed in-depth online, as well as some of the more complex things you can choose to do with the added care of this technique. We'll be only discussing the advantages and disadvantages, here.

Automatic formatting by the seller is by far the fastest method. There are very few hurdles to publishing in this way—LibreOffice or OpenOffice.Org can be used if you don't have access to MS Office products. The biggest problem is that the formatting is all default. If you don't like the way that it is done automatically, you're out of luck altogether.

You don't get to give the Amazon converter feedback, and if you're repeatedly tweaking your submission to try to achieve the perfect result, then you're already wasting all the time you saved.

Therefore, I would recommend automatic formatting for people who aren't finicky about formatting. My fiancé is incredibly finicky, and that's why he does the print formatting for my stories. But for me, I am not so finicky and I would rather get back to my real job, writing, as opposed to sitting there trying to proof things on screen, on my Kindle device, on my Android device, and so on.

On the exact opposite end of the spectrum is hand-encoding. Writing here is most easily done in a text editor (which is where I do most of my writing, personally!) with future formatting in mind. Then you encode it as HTML, write two XML files to get everything included and in the right order, and for .mobi files you run it all through Kindlegen; for .epub files you add it all to a zip archive and change the extension. This information is all available for free on the internet if you just look for "make epub by hand" and "make mobi by hand." Other sources go much more in-depth about the process and provide ample examples.

The primary advantage here is the ability to get a very specific experience for the reader. Many more traditional printing elements are easily imitated (line-and-a-half spacing between paragraphs or the first line of a chapter being non-indented, to name two examples) where automatic generators will largely ignore elements like this. Hand-conversion is much more time-consuming, but with some know-how and spending the time, a result that really stands out as very professionally-done is possible where it's not really possible with the automatic converter.

In between the two, there are tools—the most well known of which is Mobipocket Creator, which can handle mobi and epub files—that will let you edit your document in a WYSIWYG editor similar to Microsoft Word, but will put out a mobi or epub that you can use to proof before submitting the way you could with a hand-converted file.
I have heard people tell success stories of using these software packages, but I have not had any success with them when I used them. They were not much faster than hand converting (when the framework was in place: after hand-converting two stories, I made a 'template' for the XML files that shortened the entire process considerably), and didn't look much better than auto-converted titles. I do not personally consider these tools to be worthwhile and would not advocate their use.

Printing Physical Books

Realities of Printing

When I made the transition from purely digital to offering some printed titles, a number of problems appeared that had seemed trivial before. For me, this was a big surprise, as I had thought that between my fiancé and I, we'd done a lot of good work on our formatting. Months of getting back rejections on designs because there was insufficient bleed we finally figured out what they meant. I mean to spare you that trouble.

Let me first start by dispelling some possible thoughts:

You might want your text to touch the edge of your cover. Just give that up right now. There are certain realities to printing, and one of the biggest is that your book is not printed by hand, it's not cut by hand. I worked for two months in a print factory, and it didn't make me an expert but it let me see what things look like before they ship out of the factory.

Printing is done, almost always, on rolls. It's cut, later, by a roller with a sharp blade that cuts out the shape or size of the page. Almost always, this will put the cut within 1/16 inch of the target. When it doesn't, then it's a fairly noticeable problem, and most printing press operators will be able to make the adjustment if they're paying attention.

With the constant drive to cut costs, just like any other industry, printing presses are running on shrinking margins, cutting pay, and skilled operators are often running the machine much faster than they'd ideally like. Then there's the sad fact that not every printer is especially skilled.

That, basically, is why it's important to put a margin on your design. There are two margins that any reputable press will require: BLEED and TRIM. It's easy to get confused on which is which, and for a writer it's often more confusing, because most writers aren't printers or print designers. But trust me when I say this: It's for your protection, not just a hassle.

CreateSpace requires 1/8 inch trim and 1/8 inch bleed. That means that 1/8 inch is going to be left on the cutting room floor (the TRIM), and 1/8 inch is required as a margin around my entire cover (including the spine and back cover, the BLEED).

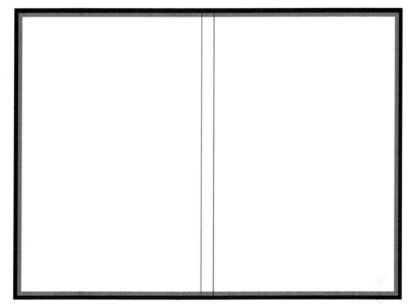

In the above example, which is to-scale for a 6x9 book, the thick black outline represents the TRIM. It will be cut off of the final printed edition, and so you shouldn't put ANYTHING in it that you want to be seen. But you want your color to extend all the way to the outermost edge. The thick gray line inside the black trim is the BLEED. You can put images there, such as stock photos and patterns and anything else you like, but do not let anything that you can't afford to lose overlap the gray border, so absolutely do not put text outside the white area. The white area is completely safe for printing purposes. That's where your text should be and that's where the focal point of your stock should be.

For our CreateSpace editions, we use a 6x9 trim size (that is to say, after the pages are cut to size the book is 6 inches wide by 9 inches tall). For a 24-page book (the minimum number of pages) that's 12.3 inches including the trim all the way across, 9.25 inches including trim tall. Each page is 0.002252 inches thick in the spine, and that is why it is not 12.25 inches.

That entire area is filled with a color that blends fairly well with the cover that we designed for digital print. Often this will be black for our darker covers, but for lighter covers it's more important to pull a color from the image.

Then the items (back-cover description, front cover at 300 dpi, and the Midnight Climax blurb that all of us include on our print editions) are placed and colors are changed to fit the overall design.

Bear in mind that while no text can be placed inside the margins, the background image (with no text) is encouraged to extend at the very least to the trim line—this is why I recommended a 75 px margin in your covers. It ensures that if, in the future, you decide to convert your back catalog to print, your margins are all correct. On our first pen-name, we found that most of our catalog was done improperly and all the covers had to be redone to comply with CreateSpace requirements.

However, it all starts with that colored canvas. For months, Nathan and I were pulling our hair out because we would submit stories to CreateSpace and they'd be returned two, sometimes three times because the PDF lacked bleed. Adding the colored background, even if it's just white, made all the difference.

There is also a certain value in marking the location where the printer is going to be placing the barcode in advance of doing any text layout on the back cover. It can be very tempting and very easy to try to balance text blocks around the idea that there's not going to be a big bar code when you don't see it sitting there. You won't need to place it yourself, it will be automatically added for you, but it needs to be taken into consideration even though you almost certainly won't be in a position to see it before you send in your cover to get proofed.

As an additional unpleasant reality of publishing via a service like CreateSpace, there are two separate proofing stages—more if changes are made. First, the entire thing has to go through a "review" process which takes a few hours; in my experience, if you submit before you go to bed, it's almost always finished with the review stage by the time you wake up. Then you have the option to proof it yourself. If there's a problem, you fix it, and then have to wait for it all to be reviewed again.

This is essentially unavoidable, however. Otherwise, there would be countless legal problems. Would-be publishers with dubious morals would get some negative comment on his or her book, and then suddenly he or she is suing CreateSpace because of a printing error that was in fact a design error, and would've been caught by robust checks.

Or CreateSpace would OK the content of a tame cover that lacks bleed, and then it's replaced with hardcore pornography because it won't be checked again.

So as much as it is frustrating for me, and I imagine it will be frustrating to you, bear in mind that there's nothing that CreateSpace or competitors could do about this problem. It, like the margins mentioned above, is a simple reality of the business.

To put it directly once more: There are some things that are worth considering as a valid form of enticement. A larger percentage of the royalty, for example, might be worth slightly lesser-quality paper. This is a decision you're going to have to make for yourself, and I recommend you try to get a sample from any prospective company that you can't get a comment on.

However, other things are simply a mark of quality. If they're not ensuring that you have a proper bleed, or that you're not providing high-quality images, then the odds are very good that they're simply trying to take your money. My experience has absolutely been that any company that allows its customers to make a fool of themselves does not take their customer base very seriously, and rarely do they provide a product that would warrant overlooking such a breach of ethics.

Printing Services

The most common option for smaller authors in self-publishing is an on-demand printing service. There are a few different providers that will charge different fees and distribute to different storefronts (both online and brick-and-mortar, for a fee), but my personal preference is CreateSpace (createspace.com) because it's an Amazon affiliate, and as a result posts all of your print titles on Amazon, where I get the majority of my sales in the first place.

Other services, which I haven't used, include:

Lulu (lulu.com)
DiggyPod (diggypod.com)

Xlibris (www2.xlibris.com)

Still other services were available at the time of writing, but either escaped my search or looked disreputable. As with all other things in life, use your instincts when evaluating any service that is going to be handling your money.

Transitioning from Digital to Print

There are a few major considerations when making a transition from digital to print:

Covers
Layout
Extra Material

Page layout is a fairly deep subject, and it's going to be covered later. Covers have a few sticking points to avoid, but otherwise are fairly easy to deal with.

First, make sure that you're using high-enough resolution covers. For a Kindle, there is no reason to go above 1280x720. Simply put, the resolution isn't there. You're wasting your time and your bandwidth and many people are going to use low-resolution images because it takes up less space on their hard drive. For printing, however, 'resolution' doesn't have as hard an upper-limit, and it is incredibly obvious when low-resolution images are used. 150 dots-per-inch is a bare minimum for good printing, and I prefer to work in higher resolution still, 300 at least. As long as your cover is high enough resolution, though (at 300 dpi, a 6x9 cover is 1800px wide and 2700px tall, hence the numbers in chapter 5) there's no major concern here.

Second, make sure you're taking into account bleed. This was mentioned in the section on cover design, so it shouldn't be a major stumbling block either. These two things are the only major problem, and in my opinion they are best practice for digital design as well.

Finally, there are a few pages of material that are not necessary, or are less-necessary for digital prints.
Cover pages are absolutely the standard in printed books. These should contain your book's title, your tags, and your name. Anything else is optional, but may include the name of any publishing group or logo.
Copyright pages are also considered standard. This is where you want to address a few things, in no particular order:

List your ISBN. It's not absolutely necessary, but it's standard.
When you print your book, it is automatically 'copyrighted' under US law. However, it's wise to put that into writing;
The format I use is 'Book Title © YEAR Dalia Daudelin' and 'This edition of Book Title © YEAR Midnight Climax'.
Any credits. This includes stock covers—even though you paid for them, you need to mention the copyright holders, or you risk a lawsuit. It's much easier to attribute now and spend a few seconds, than it is to not attribute and then spend considerable time and money fighting a legal battle.

Schools of Thought on Print Design

There's a thousand ways to format a book. People have been doing it for years, and at any given point in time there were at least three or four different ideas, and as they've developed some have been updated.

There are generally, however, two ideas on how book printing should work.

With that said, both of them are trying to do the exact same thing in different ways and their methods differ because of their different philosophies.

A book's interior layout should be approached as two open pages—not as a pair of single pages. The text is treated by most (if not all!) layout systems as conceptually being part of the same unit, and the center margins are treated as a necessity rather than an ideal.

The idea is to achieve a look where that two-block section is centered and balanced on the page, and the layout creates an appealing look. The way this is done varies from system to system.

MODERN   ·

Most modern books are designed with nearly equal margins on all sides. People grow up seeing this as the default for most of their textbooks and mass market titles and associate it with a professional style.

The primary motivation here is space efficiency. When you are your own publisher, every page you can save is a penny that you keep in your own pocket, and as the saying goes, 'a penny saved is a penny earned.'

The traditional systems of book design all have fairly healthy margins and that's fine and dandy when the paper isn't yours, but when you have to print 100,000 copies of the 2013 edition of World History, then it suddenly becomes preferable to become miserly with your paper.

With that said, it is in many ways the standard for modern book design even though I would argue (and have argued) that it is less attractive. For that reason, you might want to use a system like this because readers will be at home with the design.

TRADITIONAL

The most well-known "Canon" of page layout is the Van de Graaf Canon, established in 1946 to try to model traditional codices—not the same Van de Graaf for whom the generator is named.

There are dozens of ways that all approximate this same system. This is without a doubt the way that books have been designed since the earliest books we can find.

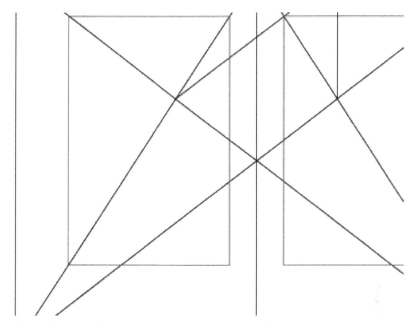

(Via Wikipedia.org, Popularized by Jan Tschichold in his
book The Form of the Book in 1975.)

CHAPTER SEVEN
Closing Remarks

A Few Things To Remember

This is a business, and your choices are going to ultimately decide how much money you're making. That can be scary, and it can even be scary when you're succeeding, not knowing what to do with yourself.

But above all, bigger than all these tips, bigger than all the points I make: You can afford to fail. If everything goes horribly wrong, then maybe Roxie Feurouge walks off into the night and reappears as Dalia Daudelin. All your mistakes, your bad ideas, are a clean slate. Now, of course, you don't want to do that unless you have to. In hindsight, I probably shouldn't have changed my name. I wouldn't have if I knew then what I know now. But even when I made that big mistake, I am still doing okay.

You don't need every story to be a huge seller. You don't need every story to make money the first month. If you keep working, you'll make the money back, and eventually you're working with a big catalog and your income is all profit, with little to no expenditure each month. The fans will come with time and hard work, and you don't need to panic if you don't have anything coming in as fast as you'd like.

Ultimately, don't slack off, but don't panic. It's going to be okay. Trust me.

Appendix
Online Resources for Writers

Storefronts

Amazon KDP: https://kdp.amazon.com/
Smashwords: https://www.smashwords.com/
Nook Press: https://www.nookpress.com/
Kobo: https://writinglife.kobobooks.com/
D2D: https://www.draft2digital.com
Google Books: http://books.google.com/googlebooks/publisher.html
Rainbow eBooks: http://www.rainbowebooks.com
All Romance eBooks: http://www.allromanceebooks.com/

Author Resources

Amazon Associates: https://affiliate-program.amazon.com/ This allows you to link to any product on Amazon and anything a customer buys, within 24 hours of clicking your link, will give you a percentage of the profits.
Amazon Author Central: https://authorcentral.amazon.com/ Allows you to group your books under your pen name for easier management, as well as allowing you to add extra information to your books.
Mailchimp: http://mailchimp.com/ The easiest way to run a mailing list. Set this up before even your first book is published!
RaffleCopter: http://www.rafflecopter.com/ This website makes it easy to set up giveaways where a random winner is picked.
Pay With A Tweet: http://www.paywithatweet.com/ If you want to offer a book for free but still gain something from it, using

Pay With A Tweet allows fans to pick up a free ebook as long as they tweet about it. Great for word of mouth!

Squarespace: http://www.squarespace.com/ If you're ready to set up your website, I recommend starting here. The website templates offered by Squarespace allow even someone who isn't tech savvy to create a beautiful and feature rich website. For an example, you can look at my own website, http://daliadaudelin.com.

Blogger: https://www.blogger.com/ A free blogging service in case you're looking for a free option for building a web presence.

Tumblr: http://www.tumblr.com/ Another free blogging service. This is one of the most popular social media websites out there right now, though it's more popular with younger demographics than most erotica is targeting.

Korner Kafe Exposed: https://www.facebook.com/KornerKafeX Free advertisement on Facebook.

What To Read After Fifty Shades of Grey: https://www.facebook.com/WhatToReadAfter50ShadesOfGrey Free advertisement on Facebook.

Blogs, Forums and Articles

These websites will teach you even more about self publishing, in general or specifically erotica, going more in depth on some of the topics discussed here.

Smutwriters.com: http://smutwriters.com/
Dean Wesley Smith's blog: http://www.deanwesleysmith.com/
Kristine Kathryn Rusch's blog: http://kriswrites.com/
A Newbie's Guide to Publishing blog: http://jakonrath.blogspot.com/

The Passive Voice blog: http://www.thepassivevoice.com/
Selena Kitt's blog: http://selenakitt.com/
Erotica Author Forum: http://eroticauthorforum.com/ (Now behind a paywall to protect the authors on the forum.)

Programs

Open Office: http://www.openoffice.org/
LibreOffice: https://www.libreoffice.org/
Scrivener: http://www.literatureandlatte.com/
Scribus: http://www.scribus.net/canvas/Scribus
GIMP: http://www.gimp.org/
Write Or Die: http://writeordie.com/
Pomodoro Time Management Software: http://en.wikipedia.org/wiki/Pomodoro_technique_software

Stock Photos

Erotic Stock Photos: http://eroticstockphotos.com/index.php
BigStockPhoto: http://www.bigstockphoto.com/
Desposit Photos: http://depositphotos.com/
IngImage: http://www.ingimage.com/
Dreamstime: http://www.dreamstime.com/
123rf: http://www.123rf.com/
RGBStock: http://www.rgbstock.com/
Canstock Photo: http://www.canstockphoto.com/
Romance Novel Covers: http://www.romancenovelcovers.com/
Hot Damn Stock: http://www.romancenovelcovers.com/

Cover Artists

PickyMe: http://pickymeartist.com/
Kanaxa: http://www.kanaxa.com/
Earthly Charms: http://www.earthlycharms.com/
Damonza: http://damonza.com/
Fiona Jayde: http://fionajaydemedia.com/
Anne Cain: http://www.annecain-art.com/
Hot Damn Designs: http://www.hotdamndesigns.com/
Book Beautiful: http://www.bookbeautiful.com/

Editors

Anne Victory: http://www.victoryediting.com/
Emily Eva Editing: http://emilyevaediting.weebly.com/
Cathleen Ross: http://www.cathleenross.com/
Book-Editing.com: http://www.book-editing.com/
Helen Hardt: http://www.helenhardt.com/editingpg.html
Sharon Muha: http://www.sharonmuha.com/
Em Petrova: http://empetrova.wordpress.com/
Infinity Publishing: http://www.infinitypublishing.com/editorial-services/

To contact the Midnight Climax authors

leave a message (646) 926-7450
or
email midnightclimaxerotica@gmail.com

61665018R00063

Made in the USA
Lexington, KY
16 March 2017